Contents

ONE of the most destructive propaganda narratives around today is the one promulgated by western liberals which holds that all the crimes Israel has been committing are a historical anomaly caused by Benjamin Netanyahu and a few far right extremists coming to power. That's false. This is what Israel has always been, from its very inception.

This is Israel. This is it. What you're looking at is the only thing Israel could ever have been. What we are seeing from Israel today is the inevitable outcome of the ethnosupremacist, hypermilitaristic, psychopathic ideology upon which the state was founded. Israel's horrific abuses in Gaza, the West Bank, Lebanon, Syria and Iran are the fruits of the tree from a seed that was planted after the second world war.

Netanyahu didn't make Israel the way it is. The way Israel is made Netanyahu. Netanyahu is Israel in its natural state.

All works are written by Caitlin Johnstone and Tim Foley. The Caitlin Johnstone project is 100 percent reader-funded. Cover is an original oil portrait of Francesca Albanese by Caitlin Johnstone.

Visit caitlinjohnst.one for the original articles and their supporting links.

This Is Israel

This is Israel. This is what the Zionist project looks like. The dead kids. The blown-out hospitals. The desperate, starving civilians. This is it.

There is no alternate version of Israel where these things are not happening. The liberal Zionist vision of a two-state solution and a just and peaceful Israel exists solely in the imaginations of the people who envision it. Nothing like it has ever existed. Everything about the modern state of Israel is unyieldingly hostile to that vision.

You either support the existence of the Israel you see before you, or you support the end of the apartheid Zionist entity. There is no hidden third option. There are no other positions on the menu. To pretend otherwise is to live in a fantasy land.

You either want to burn children alive, or you don't. You either want to deliberately starve civilians, or you don't. You either want to bomb hospitals, or you don't. You either want to deliberately assassinate Palestinian journalists while forbidding foreign journalists entry into Gaza, or you don't. You either want to deliberately massacre civilians and systematically destroy civilian infrastructure in order to force the removal of Palestinians from a Palestinian territory, or you don't. And if you don't, you must oppose the state of Israel.

That's Israel, the state. Not just Netanyahu. Not just extremist settlers. Not just "far right elements within the Israeli government".

Israel itself. Because everything we are seeing Israel do is the result of everything Israel is as a state.

Everything Israel is doing is the result of everything it has always been. As soon as the west decided to drop a settler-colonialist state on top of a pre-existing civilization wherein the new immigrants would receive preferential treatment over the indigenous inhabitants who were already living there, it became inevitable that Israel would wind up in the condition it's in today.

Because there was no way to uphold that status quo without mass displacement and nonstop tyranny, violence and abuse. There was no way to set up a tiered society where one tier is placed above the other without indoctrinating the public to accept that apartheid system by systematically dehumanizing the members of the disempowered group.

Set up a status quo of dehumanizing a group of people and manufacturing consent for violence and abuse against them, and you will inevitably wind up with a far right apartheid state which is committing genocide, as surely as dropping a stone off a building will result in a stone falling to the ground.

What we are seeing in Gaza today was baked into the state of Israel ever since its inception.

All those dead kids on your social media feed are the fruit of a tree whose seed was planted after the second world war. That tree has been bearing more and more fruit, and it will continue to for as long as it remains standing. Because that's just the kind of tree it is. The only kind of tree it ever could have been.

Saying "I support Israel but I don't support the actions of Netanyahu in Gaza" is like saying "I like this apple tree but only when it sprouts coconuts instead of apples." That is not the kind of tree it is. The apple tree will only produce apples, and the genocide tree will only produce genocide.

Israel's supporters avoid confronting obvious truths like these. Support for Israel depends on mass-scale psychological compartmentalization. Everything about it revolves around avoiding unpleasant truths instead of deeply and viscerally reckoning with them.

Averting the eyes from the video footage of Israel's atrocities in Gaza. Averting the eyes from the contradictions between the values they purport to hold and everything Israel is as a state. Averting the eyes from the mountains upon mountains of evidence staring us all in the face. That's the only way support for Israel is able to continue.

In order to become a truth-driven species, we need to stop hiding from uncomfortable truths. And one of our favorite hiding places for uncomfortable truths at this point in history is the modern state of Israel, and the western empire's support for it. •

Israel's Backers Are Now Advocating The Assassination Of Greta Thunberg
• Notes From The Edge Of The Narrative Matrix •

US Senator Lindsay Graham has just tweeted an article titled "Greta Thunberg sets sail with Gaza flotilla that aims to break Israeli naval blockade," adding the comment, "Hope Greta and her friends can swim!"

Australian Zionist think tanker Arsen Ostrovsky somehow outdid Graham, tweeting "Oh look, the little jihadi Greta Thunberg is trying to get into Gaza, to show solidarity with Hamas. It would be so sad if something were to happen to her flotilla…"

There's not a lot that can shock me about Israel and its supporters these days. But if you'd traveled back in time a few years ago it would be hard to explain to someone how we got to a timeline that includes Israel supporters openly advocating the assassination of Greta Thunberg.

•

The reason Gaza ceasefire negotiations have kept falling through under both the Biden and Trump administrations is that Israel, with the backing of the US government, keeps insisting on the right to resume its genocidal slaughter after a temporary intermission.

A big part of the problem is that this is a genocide, not a war, but all the framing is around negotiating a "ceasefire" to end the "war"

even as Israel keeps rejecting any ceasefire agreement which would require them to end the genocide.

Hamas insists on an end to the genocide, and Israel goes "No can do, but tell ya what: we can pause the war for a few weeks!" And then the mass media go "HAMAS REJECTS CEASEFIRE" while liberals go "Oh it's so sad that they can't negotiate an end to this terrible war!"

But it's not a war, it's a genocide. You can negotiate an end to a war, but you can't negotiate an end to a genocide. Israel has openly declared that the killing will continue until there are no more Palestinians left in Gaza—either by death or by ethnic cleansing. Israel wants to eliminate all Palestinians from Gaza more than it wants the remaining hostages. It wants to eliminate all Palestinians from Gaza more than it wants peace. Hamas has nothing to offer Israel that it wants more than it wants to purge Palestinians from a Palestinian territory.

If this were being treated as a genocide, all law-abiding states would interfere to force Israel to stop. But because it's being falsely treated as a "war" they just stand passively by and periodically cluck about ceasefire negotiations, thereby allowing Israel to continue its genocide.

•

The big controversy this weekend was the emergence of a sex tape featuring journalist Glenn Greenwald, which he says was released "without my knowledge or consent" and that the motive was a "maliciously political one."

After Greenwald's public statement on the matter, Twitter was flooded with commentators and members of the public from all across the political spectrum expressing their support for him, apparently nullifying whatever effect the release of the sex tape was supposed to have.

I'm going to call this a solid win for humanity.

•

The US is removing Syria from its longtime designation as a state sponsor of terrorism now that it has a puppet regime in Damascus, with US envoy Thomas Barrack proclaiming that "Thank God, the issue of state sponsor of terrorism is gone with the Assad regime being finished."

This is the US admitting that the "terrorist" designation just means "not aligned with US interests." Syria's new president was an actual ISIS and Al Qaeda official—literally the leader of Al Qaeda in Syria. But because he's US-aligned, "terrorism" is no longer a concern.

•

Our rulers did not expect this. They did not expect the public to sustain ferocious opposition to the Gaza holocaust for 20 months. In October 2023 they would've been assuring each other that all the protesting and outrage would die off soon, because that's what normally happens.

And it just didn't. People refused to let this thing fade into the background. The mass media were forced to keep reporting on it—albeit with extreme bias—because if they didn't report on it at all they'd lose their last shred of credibility in the eyes of the public, and people would keep sharing the information on their own anyway.

Remember how excited the Israel apologists got when those two embassy staff members were killed? They were like "Welp, that's it for the pro-Palestine movement! Saying Free Palestine is not allowed anymore everybody! Ahh, thank goodness, I was worried people would never let this thing go."

And it just didn't pan out that way. Nobody bought it. The embassy staff killings were shuffled off in the daily news churn and forgotten, while Gaza remained.

And I just think it's worth flagging what a miracle that is. How completely unexpected and unanticipated this would have been for our ruling institutions. They really thought we were all sufficiently ground down and subdued by life under the empire to just let them do what they want to Gaza without any resistance. And they were wrong.

There's some life left in us yet. It is not a foregone conclusion that we will just passively watch our rulers carry us off over the ledge of dystopia, ecological disaster and nuclear armageddon. Revolution is not an impossible pipe dream. There is still a spark of hope. •

Zen And The Art Of New York Times Headlines

The New York Times has just published one of the most insane headlines I have ever seen it publish, which is really saying something.

"Gaza's Deadly Aid Deliveries," the title blares.

If you were among the majority of people who only skim the headline without reading the rest of the article, you would have no idea that Israel has spent the last few days massacring starving civilians at aid sites and lying about it. You would also have no idea that it is Israel who's been starving them in the first place.

The headline is written in such a passive, amorphous way that it sounds like the aid deliveries themselves are deadly. Like the bags of flour are picking up assault rifles and firing on desperate Palestinians queuing for food or something.

The sub-headline is no better: "Israel's troops have repeatedly shot near food distribution sites."

Oh? They've shot "near" food distribution sites, have they? Could their discharging their weapons in close proximity to the aid sites possibly have something to do with the aforementioned deadliness of the aid deliveries? Are we the readers supposed to connect these two pieces of information for ourselves, or are we meant to view them as two separate data points which may or may not have anything to with one another?

The article itself makes it clear that Israel has admitted that IDF troops fired their weapons "near" people waiting for aid after they failed to respond to "warning shots", so you don't have to be Sherlock Holmes to figure out what happened here. But in mainstream publications the headlines are written by editors, not by the journalists who write the articles, so they get to frame the story in whatever way suits their propaganda agenda for the majority who never read past the headline.

We saw another amazingly manipulative New York Times headline last month, "Israeli Soldiers Fire in Air to Disperse Western Diplomats in West Bank," about the IDF firing "warning shots" at a delegation of foreign officials attempting to visit Jenin.

This was a story which provoked outcry and condemnation throughout the western world, but look at the lengths the New York Times editor went to in order to frame the IDF's actions in the most innocent way possible. They were firing into the air. They were firing "to disperse western diplomats"—like that's a thing. Like diplomats are crows on a cornfield or something. Oh yeah, ya know ya get too many diplomats flockin' around and ya gotta fire a few rounds to disperse 'em. Just normal stuff.

It's amazing how creative these freaks get when they need to publicly exonerate Israel and its western allies of their crimes. The IDF commits a war crime and suddenly these stuffy mass media editors who've never created any art in their lives transform into poets, bending and twisting the English language to come up with lines that read more like Zen koans than reporting on an important news event.

It's impossible to have too much disdain for these people. •

A Truth–Based Relationship With Reality Requires Courage

Ultimately it comes down to courage. Being brave enough to stare squarely at the horrors of Gaza. To face the harsh reality that we are ruled by monsters and our civilization is diseased. To bring our own inner darkness into the light of consciousness where it can be healed.

Coming into a truth-based relationship with reality requires courage. That's all I'm ever really talking about in this space, when all is said and done: coming into a truth-based relationship with reality, both collectively as a society and as individuals.

Because that's the only thing that can ever lead to health and harmony. The human species will never move into a healthy relationship with each other and with Earth's ecosystem as long as our behavior is driven by power-serving systems justified by indoctrinated lies and propaganda. The human individual will never know inner peace if it remains driven by unconscious inner forces and unhealed trauma.

These unwholesome dynamics are not going to correct themselves. Untruth needs to be directly confronted, both in the empire under which we live, and inside ourselves. This takes courage.

It is uncomfortable to look directly at the horrors the western empire is unleashing in Gaza, and elsewhere.

It can be scary to confront the possibility that everything you've been taught about your world and your country is a lie.

It can be extremely frightening to look deep within yourself with the intention of uncovering all the unpleasant truths you have hidden from yourself over the years.

It can be downright terrifying to seek spiritual enlightenment only to discover that it entails losing yourself and your entire world.

Lies are comforting. Truth is scary. But truth is the only way out of the dysfunction we have created for ourselves. So if we want peace, health and happiness, we're going to have to get brave.

We must look precisely where we don't want to look. We must welcome the revelations we least hope to see. We must make friends with the ugliest of truths. We must get comfortable with discomfort. That's the only way out of this mess.

The transition into a healthy and harmonious world will be a great leap into the complete unknown, because it will be a shift into something that has never existed on this planet before. That leap will not be made until we are ready to make it, come what may.

Until then we can only act in courageous service of truth, in what little ways we are able. Learn as much as we can about our world and our society, especially the parts we'd rather avoid. Speak the truth about what we are seeing, especially when our voice shakes. Bring our unconscious wounds and delusions into consciousness and enlighten that which is endarkened, especially in the ways we're most reluctant to.

Humanity can only walk into the light of truth one trembling step at a time. And we are each responsible for our own steps on that journey. •

Epstein, Israel, ISIS, Palantir
• Notes From The Edge Of The Narrative Matrix •

Amid the inevitable giant ego clash between Elon Musk and Donald Trump, Musk tweeted that the president "is in the Epstein files," saying "That is the real reason they have not been made public."

As we have discussed previously, it is a known fact that Trump is on the Epstein flight logs and has been obstructing the release of the Epstein files. It is also a known fact that Jeffrey Epstein worked with Israeli intelligence and was running a sexual blackmail operation, and that Trump has been bending over backwards to give Israel everything it wants while stomping out American free speech that is critical of Israel's actions in Gaza.

"I've known Jeff [Epstein] for fifteen years. Terrific guy," Trump said in 2002. "He's a lot of fun to be with. It is even said that he likes beautiful women as much as I do, and many of them are on the younger side."

There's no reason to take seriously anything Elon Musk says during a textbook case of narcissistic collapse, but for the record if anyone in Washington is likely to have been blackmailed by Epstein it's Donald John Trump.

•

Israel has admitted to arming ISIS-linked gangs as proxy forces in Gaza, throwing some cold water on the fuzzbrained narrative that the west is backing Israel to help defeat Islamic extremism. Israel is backing these forces in order to sow chaos and strife with the goal of advancing its ethnic cleansing objectives in the Palestinian territory.

•

Lately whenever I talk about Israel's ethnic cleansing agenda I get Israel supporters telling me "They're not doing ethnic cleansing! They're just making the Palestinians leave Gaza because they don't want them there!" Which is yet another reminder of how stupid Israel apologists are, because the forced mass expulsion of an undesired ethnic group is precisely the definition of ethnic cleansing.

•

I have this conversation every single day:

Me: Here's evidence of Israel doing something evil.

Israel supporter: All Hamas has to do is surrender and release the hostages and this ends immediately.

Me: No that's false, Israel is openly saying the slaughter will continue until all Palestinians have been ethnically cleansed from Gaza regardless of whether Hamas surrenders or the hostages are released. Here's a pile of evidence showing that this is the case.

Israel supporter: Yeah well that's what happens when you start a war you can't win. Next time don't do terrorism.

Me: You were just claiming Hamas can end this at any time by making different decisions. Now that you know Hamas is powerless to stop Israel's ethnic cleansing atrocities you have pivoted to saying all Palestinians deserve mass murder and ethnic cleansing. Sounds like you'll just support Israel no matter what it does regardless of facts or morality.

Israel supporter: ANTISEMITE ANTISEMITE ANTISEMITE ANTISEMITE

•

I keep meaning to talk about how the Trump administration is reportedly granting oligarch Peter Thiel's odious company Palantir a central role in a massive authoritarian expansion in government surveillance powers which would see American data compiled and tracked across multiple government agencies.

For those who don't know, Palantir is a CIA-backed surveillance and data mining tech company with longstanding ties to both the US intelligence cartel and to Israel, and has already been playing a crucial role in both the US empire's sprawling surveillance network and Israeli atrocities against Palestinians.

This is being framed by the political/media class as a Trump policy, but it's obviously a US empire policy. These sweeping surveillance powers are intended to remain in place long after Trump is gone, regardless of who happens to be in office.

•

We are being asked to believe that individuals becoming violently radicalized by the ongoing genocide in Gaza is of greater concern than the ongoing genocide in Gaza.

No. That isn't going to happen.

Perhaps the best way to stop people from committing acts of violence in response to the genocide in Gaza would be to cease actively fucking facilitating the fucking genocide in Gaza.

•

Palestine supporters: Here's a video that just came out showing Israel massacring Palestinian civilians again.

Israel supporters: Okay, so, two thousand years ago...

•

The world waking up to Israel's depravity reminds me of the moment I first saw how nasty and abusive my ex was. That first glimpse when I finally let myself see the sadism and ill will he had for me was the beginning of the end.

Maybe the world is beginning its own moment of clarity. •

Offending Zionists Is Good, Actually
• Notes From The Edge Of The Narrative Matrix •

British comedian Dawn French was successfully pressured into publicly apologizing for a video she made in opposition to the Gaza holocaust after Israel supporters made a stink claiming she was insensitive to Israel about October 7.

I can't believe it's 2025 and people are still worried about offending Zionists. Oh gosh I'd better issue an apology, I've upset the people who are cheerleading an active genocide. Better be careful how I word this or I might seem insensitive to people who think it's fine to bomb hospitals and burn children alive. Oh no I can't say that because if I do I'll be in hot water with the "intentionally starving civilians is good" crowd.

Fuck these freaks. Fuck 'em. The more butt hurt they are by the things you say, the better. It is good for evil people who desire evil things to be upset by your words and deeds. The more Israel's supporters hate you, the more likely it is that you are a decent person. Say what needs saying and wear their outrage as a badge of honor.

•

Israel killed four journalists in an airstrike on a hospital the other day, and it caused barely a blip in the news cycle. It's so crazy how this is just normal now.

This was at the Al-Ahli Arab Baptist Hospital by the way, which you may remember as the hospital that Israel ferociously denied bombing at the beginning of its onslaught in October 2023. Israel has since bombed that very same hospital many times.

The behavior of the state of Israel is one nonstop argument against the continued existence of the state of Israel.

•

Most Israel apologia is just saying ridiculous nonsense in an assertive tone and demanding to be taken seriously. They're butchering children by the thousands in a completely undisguised effort to purge all Palestinians from a Palestinian territory, and then spouting a bunch of transparently bogus talking points to try and spin this as fine and normal. But because mainstream institutions solemnly promote this obvious bullshit, we're expected to treat it like it's a completely valid position that needs to be respected.

There's no actual basis for the pro-genocide position in truth, logic, or morality. It's a completely indefensible position, so self-evidently wrong that a child could recognize it at a glance. But because support for Israel is so entrenched within our political-media class, and because Israel's supporters have a solid understanding of the power of narrative control, they are able to promote this nakedly evil agenda by sheer force of will — just by saying their talking points in confident-sounding voices.

It's mostly just about tone. They have no arguments, so they rely heavily on authoritatively stated assertions, condescension, and rote repetition of the same tired slogans over and over again.

Such tactics are why so many westerners still believe Israel-Palestine is much too complicated an issue for them to take a solid position on. They see pundits and politicians defending Israel using smug, know-it-all mannerisms all throughout the political and media landscape, so they assume there must be more to this thing than it appears at first glance. If they just stuck with their initial intuition they'd wind up siding with Palestine, but the forceful feigned self-assuredness of Israel supporters shuts them down and shuts them up.

•

It's so silly how western conservatives pretend they support Israel because they want to stand with a historically persecuted religious group when we all know it's really because they hate Muslims. They see Jews as white so in their minds they're supporting the white people against the brown people. It's nothing grander or more noble than garden variety racism.

Seems like a lot of western Jews don't understand that in the eyes of the average westerner they're literally just white people. The Jewish people we run into in the west look, speak and act pretty much the same as any other pale-skinned individual in western society, so they're not othered in the way some races and cultures are. Being Jewish isn't typically seen as any more remarkable or exotic than being Episcopalian.

This is why Jewish Zionists get the response they get from western Palestine supporters on the left. Their crying and histrionics about how the pro-Palestine protesters make their feelings feel looks exactly the same as any other white person Karening and drama queening because their feelings aren't being given priority over the lives and rights of others. It's also why Jewish anti-Zionists who spend their energy tone-policing the pro-Palestine movement tend to get a lot of pushback; for many people it reads the same as a white activist centering themselves within the Black Lives Matter movement.

Western Jews are generally seen as white people by western society. It didn't used to be that way back before our society got a lot more secular, but that's how it is now. Western Jews enjoy white privilege and do not encounter the same obstacles that actual oppressed minorities encounter in life, but the tradeoff is that when they try to act like they're an oppressed minority in order to promote the interests of Israel, people tend to scoff and roll their eyes as much as they would at any other white person acting like their whiteness makes them a disempowered victim.

There is no antisemitism epidemic in our society. There is some hatred toward Jews on the fringes, but it's nothing like the systemic prejudice people from other races and marginalized groups encounter in the west. Overwhelmingly "antisemitism" is just a victim-LARPing narrative used to bludgeon all opposition to a genocidal apartheid state whose crimes western governments have been backing to the hilt. •

Sky News Smears Greta Thunberg As A Nazi To Justify IDF Attack

IDF troops have raided the Madleen, a sailboat that was carrying aid intended to break the Israeli siege on Gaza. Everyone onboard has reportedly been abducted by Israeli forces, including climate activist Greta Thunberg.

Ahead of the abduction, a senior Israeli official told Israel's Channel 12 News that the decision had been made to stop the ship from reaching Gaza because if it was allowed through, a "wave of flotillas" would come to challenge the blockade.

This is a developing news story as of this writing with a lot more information yet to emerge. But one thing I'd like to quickly flag here is that shortly before the IDF raided the Madleen, Sky News host Jonathan Samuels strongly implied that the ship deserved to be attacked because it is full of antisemites and Hamas supporters.

During a contentious interview with Israeli journalist Gideon Levy, who voiced support for the Madleen, Samuels objected that Thunberg has been accused of antisemitism and her fellow passengers have been accused of being Hamas sympathizers, and are therefore not innocent.

"Are you sure, Jonathan, that Israel has the moral right to prevent Gaza from such a mission?" asked Levy. "I mean, from where do we take this chutzpah, as we say in Hebrew, to put this closure on Gaza even from innocent people like Greta Thunberg and her friends?"

"Yeah, perhaps the criticism is that she's not as innocent as all that," Samuels countered. "She's been accused of being antisemitic hasn't she? And there are others on board accused of being Hamas sympathizers. Therefore it could potentially be a very dangerous situation and they're quite naive to get into it, aren't they?"

By the way, the accusation of "being antisemitic" which Samuels appears to be referring to here is the single dumbest antisemitism smear that I have ever seen in my entire life.

Back in October 2023, Thunberg appeared in a photo holding a "Stand with Gaza" sign, causing furious backlash from the pro-Israel crowd. Eventually someone found an excuse to spin this as an anti-Jewish hate crime by pointing out that there was a small octopus plushie in the photo, claiming that the octopus is a some kind of antisemitic trope.

Thunberg, who has autism, then deleted the photo, saying, "It has come to my knowledge that the stuffed animal shown in my earlier post can be interpreted as a symbol for antisemitism, which I was completely unaware of. The toy in the picture is a tool often used by autistic people as a way to communicate feelings. We are of course against any type of discrimination, and condemn antisemitism in all forms and shapes. This is non-negotiable. That is why I deleted the last post."

And it was THIS insanely absurd accusation that was the basis for Jonathan Samuels smearing Greta Thunberg to justify the Israeli military attacking the ship she was on.

To be clear, this demented Israel apologia was spouted before Israel took action against the aid ship. We didn't know if Israel would raid the ship, bomb it right out of the water, or shoot everyone on board. Samuels was preemptively justifying whatever it was Israel was about to do, including mass murder on yet another Gaza aid ship.

Literally everyone who has ever publicly criticized Israel in the western world has been accused of antisemitism and being a Hamas sympathizer. If you have any kind of audience and criticize Israel's mass atrocities in Gaza to any extent, it is absolutely inevitable that you will receive those accusations. The fact that a Sky News anchor would cite such accusations as justification for Israel attacking and potentially killing someone means that, at least in the eyes of Jonathan Samuels, anyone who criticizes Israel deserves to be murdered.

Israel apologists were already advocating an attack on the Madleen, and mass media spinmeisters were already smearing its passengers as deserving of an attack. And now that the attack has happened, the information ecosystem is being bombarded by Israel supporters trying to argue that it is actually good and normal to kidnap activists who are trying to bring aid to a starving and besieged civilian population.

This shows you that there is nothing Israel could do that these freaks would not defend. It shows you who these people are. It shows you that every argument you've ever heard in support of Israel is not based on facts or morality or logic, but solely on the desire to promote the information interests of a genocidal apartheid state. It tells you everything you need to know about Israel apologia in general.

Support for Israel has no basis in truth. It has no basis in ethics or rationality. It's just a bunch of horrible people murdering, tyrannizing and stealing with the aim of conquest and domination, and then using words to justify those actions. Israel and its apologists will say whatever words they need to say in order to advance their goals of ethnic cleansing and expansionism, with no regard for what is right and what is true.

It's just a bunch of noise. You could mentally translate every word of every Israel apologist into shrieking gibberish without missing anything meaningful, because there's no actual content in it. It's just people doing evil things and then making a bunch of mouth noises to stop anyone from opposing their actions. •

After Denying Massacring Civilians Seeking Aid, Israel Routinely Massacres Civilians Seeking Aid

At the beginning of this month, Israel and its apologists ferociously denied claims that IDF troops had fired upon civilians seeking aid at a Gaza Humanitarian Foundation (GHF) site, killing 31 people.

On the second of June, Israeli forces again opened fire on civilians seeking aid in Gaza, killing three people and injuring more than 30.

On June 3, Israeli forces again opened fire on civilians seeking aid, reportedly killing at least 27 people.

The US/Israeli-backed GHF temporarily suspended operations after this spate of mass shootings.

On June 8, Israeli forces again fired upon civilians seeking aid at two separate distribution points in Gaza, killing twelve.

On June 9, Israel and Israeli-backed forces opened fire on a crowd at an aid site in Gaza, killing 14.

And on June 10, at least 36 people were reported killed and 208 wounded when Israeli forces again fired on crowds seeking aid in Gaza.

Since May 27, some 160 people have reportedly been killed in massacres at these GHF sites, which people in Gaza are reportedly beginning to refer to as a "death trap".

Think about how desperate and starving you'd have to be before you'd go seek food from people who you know will probably start spraying the crowd with bullets at some point. This really gives you an idea of how badly the people of Gaza have been suffering.

But, again, at the beginning of the month, Israel and its spinmeisters were crying antisemitic blood libel at the very suggestion that IDF troops would fire upon people trying to obtain food.

The Israeli Ministry of Foreign Affairs published a deceitful video clip which it falsely claimed showed Hamas members, not the IDF, firing on the crowd.

Netanyahu advisor Caroline Glick and Israel's "Minister of Diaspora and Combating Antisemitism" Amichai Chikli both called the reporting on the June 1 massacre a "blood libel".

White House Press Secretary Karoline Leavitt falsely accused the BBC of peddling Hamas propaganda for reporting on the June 1 massacre.

Former Israeli prime minister Naftali Bennet shared a video clip of people in Gaza not being shot at some point and claimed this proves nobody was shot at the specified incident on June 1, saying "When it's about Israel, all slander works."

The Jerusalem Post published an article titled "Media blood libel over alleged Gaza aid shooting will have far-reaching repercussions."

Israel's official Twitter account called the reporting "Hamas propaganda".

The Washington Post bowed to pressure and retracted its article on the June 1 massacre, saying it didn't "give proper weight to Israel's denial and gave improper certitude about what was known about any Israeli role in the shootings."

Then, a few days later, CNN published a report based on extensive video analysis and eyewitness interviews which found that all evidence, contrary to Israel's claims, "points to the Israeli military opening fire on crowds of Palestinians as they tried to make their way to the fenced enclosure to get food."

Even without the CNN report, Israel's own actions since June 1 have proved that Israeli forces do indeed deliberately fire upon starving civilians seeking humanitarian aid. Israel lied. Again.

Which should come as no surprise to anyone who's been paying attention to Israel's mass atrocities in Gaza. This is after all the same genocidal state which indignantly objected to claims that it would ever bomb a medical facility after an explosion at the Al-Ahli Arab Baptist Hospital in October 2023, only to bomb that exact same hospital many times thereafter while deliberately destroying Gaza's entire healthcare infrastructure.

One of the craziest phrases you can possibly utter in the year 2025 is "Let's give Israel the benefit of the doubt on this one." They've been caught lying so many times that there is no reason to take any of their denials seriously. You don't get to ban journalists from Gaza while getting caught lying about your actions over and over again and then have people give any weight to your denials of reported atrocities. That's not a thing. •

Staring Down The Barrel Of War With Iran Once Again

Well it looks like the US is on the precipice of war with Iran again.

US officials are telling the press that they anticipate a potential impending Israeli attack on Iran while the family members of US military personnel are being assisted with evacuation from bases in the region.

This comes as Tehran issues a warning that it will strike all US military bases within range of its missiles if it comes under attack. There are reportedly some 50,000 US troops in 10 bases which could come under fire should this occur.

The US is also evacuating its embassy in Iraq, and has authorized the departure of non-essential personnel from its embassies in Kuwait and Bahrain.

Asked by the press about the evacuations, President Trump said, "They are being moved out because it could be a dangerous place, and we'll see what happens. We've given notice to move out."

Trump is openly declaring a willingness to strike Iran if nuclear negotiations fall through, while saying he is now "much less confident" that any deal will be made.

"If they don't make a deal, they're not gonna have a nuclear weapon; if they do make a deal they're not gonna have a nuclear weapon too,"

the president said in an interview published on Wednesday, adding that "it would be nicer to do it without warfare, without people dying."

If the US backs an Israeli attack on Iran and then Iran retaliates by killing a bunch of US military personnel, we could be looking at a full-scale direct war between the US and Iran.

As I've said in this space many times before, this would be the absolute worst-case nightmare scenario for the middle east, unleashing horrors that dwarf all the other terrible abuses currently happening in the region. As Trump's now-Director of National Intelligence Tulsi Gabbard said in 2019 (back when she publicly opposed Trump's warmongering), "What is important that the American people know is a war with Iran would make the war in Iraq look like a cakewalk."

It's so stupid that this keeps happening. This could all be avoided by the US simply ceasing to support the genocidal apartheid state of Israel no matter what it does. The fact that Washington has continued to pour weapons into Israel despite all its warmongering and genocide since 2023 means the US supports everything that Israel has been doing.

If a war with Iran does occur, you will doubtless hear western pundits and politicians trying to spin this as America getting "drawn into" another war in the middle east, or Trump being tricked or manipulated into war. But

make no mistake: the US could have turned away from this path at any time, and still can.

If this Pandora's box is opened, it will be because the US empire knowingly chose to open it. •

Israel Is Bombing Iran. Here Are Some Future New York Times Headlines.

Israel has launched an extensive series of airstrikes on Iran.

The western media are of course unquestioningly regurgitating the Israeli government's evidence-free claim that these strikes were "preemptive".

The Trump regime is attempting to spin this as a completely unilateral Israeli attack which had nothing to do with the United States — a claim you could be forgiven for believing if you were born yesterday.

Here's a list of future headlines we can expect from The New York Times:

- *Iranian strikes rock Israel in unprovoked attack.*

- *Israeli families take shelter amid antisemitic terror bombing.*

- *Israeli defense minister: U.S. campus protesters somehow knew about Iranian strikes in advance, indicating Tehran coordination.*

- *Trump privately voices frustration with Netanyahu over Iran conflict the U.S. is just passively, innocently witnessing.*

- *American Jews feeling anxious, unsupported amid spiraling wars in the Middle East.*

- *Opinion: I feared for my life during airstrikes on Tel Aviv. Nobody in the world can possibly understand what this is like.*

- *Opinion: Is the U.S. at risk of being drawn into another Middle Eastern war?*

- *Opinion: Is the U.S. stumbling into another Middle Eastern war?*

- *Opinion: Is the U.S. accidentally oopsie poopsie bungling into another Middle Eastern war?*

- *Opinion: Is the U.S. being dragged kicking and screaming into a war in the Middle East, something it historically tries to avoid at all cost?*

- *US launches strikes on Iran in preemptive attack.*

- *Opinion: Is the U.S. being sucked into a third world war?*

- *Opinion: Is the U.S. tumbling headlong into a nuclear exchange with Russia and China?*

- *Opinion: The sky is darkening as nuclear radiation creeps across our land, so we must all come together and condemn Hamas.*

- *Opinion: The earth is a barren wasteland. Nothing remains. Check on your Jewish friends.* ·

While The Waymos Burn

While the Waymos burn

While the air over LA fills with smoke and teargas and Reaper drones

While Israelis hand each other trophies for not murdering Greta Thunberg

While Palantir stocks soar and insect populations plummet

While the news man writes headlines with increasingly creative phrasing

While people with nothing to lose sharpen guillotine blades

While the bank boys ask why the robot armies aren't ready yet

While keffiyeh-clad heroes march to Gaza

While secret saints work secret miracles in the margins

While a sleeping giant stirs within our depths

While the flames dance in Buddha's eyes

While my peacock feather heart opens like a fuchsia bud

While the tears roll down my cheeks for the dead and the dying

While the firelight dances on my walls and the rebels dance in the fire

I open my strange palms to our strange future and welcome it

Come what may.

•

Refresher On The Rules For Discussing Israeli Wars

Okay it's been a few months since the last war Israel started, so now that Iran's on the chopping block let's go over the rules once again.

Rule 1: Israel is never the aggressor. If Israel attacks someone it's either a response to an aggression that happened in the past, or a preemptive attack to thwart an imminent aggression in the future.

Rule 2: History automatically restarts at the date of the last act of aggression against Israel. If someone attacks Israel it was completely unprovoked, because nothing happened before the attack on Israel.

Rule 3: Anything bad that Israel does is justified by Rule 2. This is true even if it does things that would be considered completely unjustifiable if it were done by a nation like Russia or China.

Rule 4: Israel has a right to defend itself, but nobody else does.

Rule 5: Israel never bombs civilians, it bombs Bad Guys. If shocking numbers of civilians die it's because they were actually Bad Guys, or because Bad Guys killed them, or because a Bad Guy stood too close to them. If none of those reasons apply then it's for some other mysterious reason we are still waiting for the IDF to investigate.

Rule 6: Criticizing anything Israel does means you hate Jewish people. There is no other possible reason for anyone to oppose acts of mass military slaughter besides a seething, obsessive hatred for a small Abrahamic faith.

Rule 7: Nothing Israel does is ever as bad as the hateful criticisms described in Rule 6. Criticisms of Israel's actions are always worse than Israel's actions themselves, because those critics hate Jews and wish to commit another Holocaust. Preventing this must consume 100 percent of our political energy and attention.

Rule 8: Israelis are only ever the victims and never the victimizers. If Israelis kill Iranians, it's because the Iranians hate Jews. If Iranians kill Israelis, it's because the Iranians hate Jews. Israel is an innocent little lamb that just wants to mind its own business in peace.

Rule 9: The fact that Israel is literally always in a state of war with its neighbors and with displaced indigenous populations must be interpreted as proof that Rule 8 is true instead of proof that Rule 8 is ridiculous nonsense.

Rule 10: The lives of people in Muslim nations are much, much less important to us than western lives or Israeli lives. Nobody is allowed to think too hard about why this might be.

Rule 11: The media always tell the truth about Israel and its various conflicts. If you doubt this then you are likely in violation of Rule 6.

Rule 12: Unsubstantiated claims which portray Israel's enemies in a negative light may be reported as factual news stories without any fact checking or qualifications, while extensively evidenced records of Israeli criminality must be reported on with extreme skepticism and doubtful qualifiers like "Iran claims", "Hezbollah says" or "according to the Hamas-run health ministry". This is important to do because otherwise you might get accused of being a propagandist.

Rule 13: Israel must continue to exist in its current iteration no matter what it costs or how many people need to die. There is no need to present any logically or morally grounded reasons why this is the case. If you dispute this then you are likely in violation of Rule 6.

Rule 14: The US government has never lied about anything ever, and is always on the right side of every conflict.

Rule 15: Israel is the last bastion of freedom and democracy in the middle east and therefore must be defended, no matter how many journalists it has to assassinate, no matter how many press institutions it needs to shut down, no matter how many protests its supporters need to dismantle, no matter how much free speech it needs to eliminate, no matter how many civil rights its western backers need to erase, and no matter how many elections its lobbyists need to buy. •

Israel's Own Actions Invalidate All Pro-Israel Arguments

I didn't make Israel be this way. It's not my fault that this is what the Zionist project looks like. You can call me an antisemitic monster all day for criticizing Israel's genocidal atrocities and insane warmongering, but I didn't force this on Israel. This is what Israel chose to be. This is what a state full of Zionists looks like when you let the Zionists do everything they want to do.

You can talk all you want about the historic persecution of the Jewish people. You can try to argue that Jews for some reason need a state that's all their own in the geographic location where Jewish people used to live back in ancient history. But what we see before us today is what it looks like when that occurs. This is it. This is the result. This is the only result on offer. And it isn't my fault that that's the case.

All arguments made in defense of Israel ultimately rest on the unquestioned assumption that the Jewish people must definitely have a homeland where Jewish people are in control, and that this homeland must definitely be in the location that Israel is in right now. Once you accept this premise, then all the other arguments for the necessity of Israel's actions make sense and can be defended.

But we've seen the results of what that premise entails. It necessarily means nonstop violence, tyranny, war and abuse. It necessarily means genocide. It necessarily means ethnic cleansing. How do we know it necessarily means that? Because here we are.

So the premise upon which all pro-Israel arguments rest is invalid.

Which means all the arguments are baseless.

Which means there's really no good reason to keep maintaining the status quo of modern Israel.

Which means there's no good reason western government's should keep supporting that status quo.

Which means there's no good reason not to end the apartheid state, give equal rights to all, grant Palestinians the right of return, right the wrongs of the past, and have Israel and its western backers pay so many reparations to their victims that future generations will not feel the effects of their abuses.

That is the only logical position here. Israel's own actions have made that clear. Israel's critics didn't force Israel to choose those actions. Those actions are just the product of everything Israel is. •

We Are, Of Course, Being Lied To About Iran

Iran and Israel are at war, with the US already intimately involved and likely to become more so. Which of course means we'll be spending the foreseeable future getting bashed in the face with lies from the most powerful people in the world.

The most immediately obvious of these is the Netanyahu-promoted narrative that Israel initiated this conflict because Iran was on the brink of developing a nuclear weapon. With absolutely no self-consciousness or sense of irony, the Israeli prime minister followed the attacks with a statement accusing Iran of "genocidal rhetoric" which it has backed up "with a program to develop nuclear weapons." Israel, as we all know, has an unacknowledged nuclear arsenal, and its leaders are presently committing genocide in Gaza while spouting genocidal rhetoric.

"And if not stopped, Iran could produce a nuclear weapon in a very short time," Netanyahu claimed. "It could be a year. It could be within a few months — less than a year. This is a clear and present danger to Israel's very survival."

The western political/media class have been dutifully promoting this line and uncritically parroting Israel's claim that its unprovoked attack on Iran was "preemptive", but there is

absolutely no evidence that any of this is true.

Benjamin Netanyahu has spent literally decades falsely claiming that Iran was a year or two away from developing a nuke, only to have the calendar prove him wrong with the passage of time over and over again.

US intelligence chief Tulsi Gabbard testified just weeks ago that "The IC [Intelligence Community] continues to assess that Iran is not building a nuclear weapon and Supreme Leader Khamenei has not authorized the nuclear weapons program he suspended in 2003."

As journalist Séamus Malekafzali recently noted on Twitter, one of the strongest arguments that Iran had not reversed its decision to refrain from obtaining nuclear weapons is that Iranian nuclear scientists have been publicly expressing frustration about the fact that their government won't allow them to construct a nuke. They want to do it, but Tehran won't let them.

US Secretary of Defense Pete Hegseth helped pave the way for Netanyahu's claims this past Wednesday when he told the Senate that "there have been plenty of indications" Iran has been "moving their way toward something that would look a lot like a nuclear weapon."

This claim by Hegseth was swiftly scooped up and promoted by warmongers like Tom Cotton who said that Hegseth had "confirmed that Iran's terrorist regime is actively working towards a nuclear weapon."

Cotton's claim was then picked up by war pundit Mark Levin, who has been personally lobbying Trump to green light an attack on Iran, sarcastically quipping on Twitter, "So, SecDef Hegseth must by lying, too. Everyone's lying except the isolationists, Koch-heads, Islamists, Chatsworth Qatarlson and their media propagandists."

But let's back up and look at what Hegseth actually said. He did not say "Iran is building a nuclear weapon." He said "there have been plenty of indications" Iran has been "moving their way toward something that would look a lot like a nuclear weapon."

If the US had intelligence that Iran was building a nuke, Hegseth would have just said so. But instead he performed this freakish verbal gymnastics stunt muttering about indications of something that might kinda sorta *look like* a nuclear weapon, which his fellow Iran hawks then falsely took and ran with as a positive assertion that Iran was building a nuke.

There are other lies being circulated to help market this war as well. As Moon of Alabama notes, the Washington Post's odious war propagandist David Ignatius is pushing the narrative that Iran has been cultivating a relationship with de-facto al-Qaeda leader Saif al-Adel. The lie that Saddam Hussein was in league with al-Qaeda was used two decades ago to sell the invasion of Iraq.

At the same time, Trumpian pundits are currently circulating the narrative that the United States is full of Iranian "sleeper cells" who could activate at any moment and begin attacking Americans. The most egregious of these is Laura Loomer's repeated claims that there are "millions" of such cells awaiting Iran's orders to strike — possibly the single most bat shit insane claim I have ever seen anyone with any major platform make, since it would mean a very sizable percentage of the US population is actually a secret Iranian proxy army.

The fountain of lies is just getting started. There will be more. Believe nothing unless it is substantiated by mountains of evidence. These freaks have been caught lying to sell wars to the public far too many times for any of their claims to be taken on faith. •

George Dubya Trump Seeks Regime Change In Iran

President Trump has a new post on Truth Social that reads as follows:

"It's not politically correct to use the term, 'Regime Change,' but if the current Iranian Regime is unable to MAKE IRAN GREAT AGAIN, why wouldn't there be a Regime change??? MIGA!!!"

Lots to unpack here.

First of all, I love how he opens with "It's not politically correct" to support US regime change interventionism. Right away he's trying to frame support for longstanding neoconservative war agendas as part of the American right's culture war against progressivism. He's telling his base that they are actually resisting the Woke Agenda by siding with warmongering swamp monsters like Bill Kristol and John Bolton on the issue of regime change war with Iran.

Secondly, Trump's endorsement of regime change comes hours after officials from his own administration asserted emphatically that the president is not seeking regime change in Iran. Vice President JD Vance told the press that the administration "has been very clear that we don't want a regime change," and Defense Secretary Pete Hegseth said Trump's aggressions toward Iran are "not about regime change" — only to have Trump grab his phone and immediately turn them into liars.

Another interesting choice is Trump's use of the acronym "MIGA", which here is intended to stand for "Make Iran Great Again", but has for years been used by anti-Israel rightists in the United States for " Make Israel Great Again" in mockery of the Israel-first sentiments within the greater MAGA movement. That he would post this acronym at the height of criticisms that his administration is bought and owned by Israel is either a sign of being extremely out of touch or an effort to manipulate search results on Google.

Trump's post delighted arch neocon Bill Kristol, who tweeted "brb — starting up PNAC again" in response. PNAC stands for Project for the New American Century, the neoconservative think tank co-founded by Kristol which is notorious for its role in pushing Washington toward war with Iraq.

This is Trump communicating to his hardcore loyalists that it's time to start cheerleading for regime change interventionism in Iran. He's rolling out the George W Bush playbook for regime change war and playing it note for note, while still trying to ride the support he garnered with his populist messaging about draining the swamp and ending the wars. Now here he is, being applauded by the worst swamp creatures in Washington and trying to drum up consent for one of the worst wars imaginable.

Call him George Dubya Trump. •

This Was All So Very Avoidable
• Notes From The Edge Of The Narrative Matrix •

This was all so, so avoidable. The US and Israel sprinted straight at this war, cruising past off-ramp after off-ramp. The Iran nuclear deal was working as intended. Israel could have negotiated an agreement with the Palestinians, thereby cooling things off with both the Palestinian resistance and with Hezbollah long before October 7. The US empire didn't have to insist on hegemonic control over the entire region.

There was no good reason there couldn't have been peace. It was right there, ripe for the picking. Begging to be picked. Practically leaping into our hands. It was only by the most tenacious of efforts by the very worst people in the world that we wound up here. It is only by those same efforts by those same terrible people that we continue along this horrifying trajectory instead of taking the final off-ramp.

Peace is still there for the taking. It's being actively sabotaged by the very worst among us.

•

Obama's Iran deal was working. It was working. Iran was still challenging US/Israeli hegemony in the region, but it wasn't building a nuke and was following the rules. And Trump shredded it to start all this shit. It was never about nukes, it's about dominating the middle east.

•

Remember Americans, you're getting sicker and poorer as your government deprives you of even the bare minimum social safety nets people in other countries get to have while sending in the marines to quash protests in LA, so it's important that you get very, very angry at Iran.

•

Watching the internet's glee at Israel getting smashed with missiles is like watching the internet's glee at that Irishman beating up that Israeli cage fighter the other day, but with two whole countries.

Imagine living in a nation that's so evil and reviled that people love watching you get hit.

•

24

I have never in my life been more worried about a coming false flag attack than I am right now. There are powers who will easily have the means, motive and opportunity to pull off such an operation in order to drum up support for the US entering Israel's war.

•

When Israel started bombing Iran I wrote a piece joking that The New York Times was about to publish a bunch of articles about antisemitism and what an innocent little victim Israel is. Today, as a nightmare military conflict unfolds that Israel started without any provocation whatsoever, The New York Times editorial board has published an article titled "Antisemitism Is an Urgent Problem. Too Many People Are Making Excuses."

You really can't satirize these freaks.

•

Israel isn't just exposing itself, it's exposing its supporters. It's showing us that we're surrounded by psychopaths who think genocide is fine. Friends. Family members. Coworkers. They all have a big fat "I WOULD'VE SUPPORTED HITLER IN NAZI GERMANY" sign around their necks now.

•

The closest most Trumpists ever get to opposing war with Iran is "It's not our fight and we should stay out of it," which is just imaginary nonsense. Everything that's happening right now is happening precisely BECAUSE the US is involved in Israel's wars. The US is involved PRESENTLY. To say "It's not our fight and we should stay out of it" is to take your stand in an imaginary fantasy land where the US hasn't been balls deep inside Israel's warmongering this entire time.

The US has spent the last two years pouring weapons into Israel and bolstering its air defenses to help it attack its neighbors with impunity. Israeli intelligence services operate hand in glove with US intelligence services. The Pentagon is moving two destroyers toward the eastern Mediterranean as you read this.

The actual antiwar position for Americans is not telling the US government to stay out of Israel's wars, it's telling the US government to GET out of Israel's wars. Telling it to stop helping Israel inflict the mass military violence it is inflicting with increasing recklessness in ways which threaten to wreck the global economy and plunge the entire region into chaos and instability for generations.

The challenge isn't KEEPING the US out of Israel's wars, it's GETTING the US out of Israel's wars. THAT is where the push should be. •

Fox News Just Helped Netanyahu Spread The Lie That Iran Tried To Assassinate Trump

Benjamin Netanyahu was given a platform to spout lies and war propaganda on Fox News in an interview with a groveling Bret Baier, who not only allowed the Israeli prime minister's lies to cruise by unchecked but actually invited him to expand upon them.

Netanyahu promoted countless incendiary falsehoods and unsubstantiated claims throughout the interview, including the assertion that Iran was working on producing nuclear weapons and intended to give them to Yemen's Houthis to facilitate global terrorism, and that Iran was working on intercontinental ballistic missiles to nuke the east coast of the United States as well.

Perhaps the most ridiculous and brazenly propagandistic claim advanced by Netanyahu was that Iran had twice attempted to assassinate the president of the United States.

"These are people who chant 'Death to America.' They've tried to assassinate President Trump twice," said the prime minister.

Rather than push back on this claim or point out that there's been no reported evidence that any such thing has occurred, Baier instead offered Netanyahu the opportunity to drive the narrative home further

with claims of secret intelligence about these alleged assassination plots.

"You just said Iran tried to assassinate President Trump twice," Baier said. "Do you have intel that the assassination attempts on President Trump were directly from Iran?"

"Through proxies, yes, through their intel, yes, they want to kill him," Netanyahu asserted.

Netanyahu had previously made this claim on his own platform in a statement on Friday wishing President Trump a happy birthday, and now he's carrying it into the mainstream news media of the United States.

Netanyahu's claim has already been repeated in outlets like The New York Post, Washington Examiner, Breitbart, and The Independent. So it's in the blood stream now. The information ecosystem of US politics has already been infected with the virus.

It says so much about how comfortable Israel is with lying and how eager the western media are to help promote those lies that Netanyahu could go on Fox News and just casually assert that Iran "tried to assassinate President Trump twice," only to have the Murdoch muppet host invite him to expound upon this assertion rather than challenging the Israeli prime minister's evidence-free claim.

Netanyahu was fully aware that he was lying, and Baier was fully aware that Netanyahu was lying. They collaborated to push this lie before Fox News' aging audience without the faintest whisper of journalistic ethics anywhere to be heard, knowing that this one baseless assertion would help turn their Trump-sympathizing viewers toward supporting a US attack on Iran.

If you weren't around for the lead-up to the invasion of Iraq, this is what it was like. Brazen lies with a fully complicit media, with the most frenetic war propaganda circulated by the Murdoch press.

Rupert Murdoch is intimately intertwined with Israel's political elite and has a financial stake in Israeli energy which depends on Israel's ongoing military occupation of the Golan Heights. Murdoch largely has the assistance of the US government to thank for his mass media empire. He personally funded the political career of Benjamin Netanyahu, who in 2002 told the US Congress that "There is no question whatsoever that Saddam [Hussein] is seeking, is working, is advancing towards to the development of nuclear weapons," and that "If you take out Saddam, Saddam's regime, I guarantee you that it will have enormous positive reverberations on the region."

The US does not have a free press, and neither do any of its allies in the western world. Under the western power alliance the mass media operate as the propaganda services of the US-centralized empire, and the public is fed whatever narratives serve the information interests of that empire.

The lies about Iran are just getting started. There will be more. Don't buy into any part of this scam. •

If It's To Be War With Iran, Let It Be The War That Nobody Comes To

Let's make this clear: if the US bombs Iran, Iran will likely kill US military personnel in response. If this happens, it will not be Iran's fault that those military personnel died. It will be Trump's fault. It will be the fault of everyone whose decisions led to the attack which resulted in their deaths.

And they will have died for nothing.

Anyone who dies in a war with Iran will have died for nothing.

They will not have died fighting for anyone's freedom. They will not have died protecting their country.

The warmongers and propagandists will try to spin their deaths in this way, but they will be lying.

The bereaved parents and partners of those who died will also try to frame their deaths in this way, but they will only be fooling themselves, because the truth will be too painful to bear.

And the truth is that everyone who dies in such a war will have died because a few powerful people made some extremely evil decisions out of their own self-interest. And for no other reason.

Do NOT join the US military. Do NOT join the militaries of any nation which normally participates in America's wars. If you are in those militaries, you should get out by any means necessary, as quickly as possible. If further on down the track there is a draft for a war with Iran, you should dodge the draft. Because otherwise you will be throwing yourself into a war against one of the world's most formidable militaries, for nothing.

If you fight in such a war, you will be fighting for nothing.

If you die in such a war, you will die for nothing.

If you lose your limbs in such a war, you will lose your limbs for nothing.

If you suffer permanent brain damage in such a war, you will lose your mind for nothing.

Even if you manage to survive such a war with your body and brain intact, you will live the rest of your life with the knowledge that you killed human beings for nothing.

There's a stanza from Carl Sandburg's "The People, Yes" which has been bubbling around in my consciousness a lot lately:

The little girl saw her first troop parade and asked,
'What are those?'
'Soldiers.'
'What are soldiers?'
'They are for war. They fight and each tries to kill as many of the other side as he can.'
The girl held still and studied.
'Do you know ... I know something?'
'Yes, what is it you know?'
'Sometime they'll give a war and nobody will come.'

If the US directly attacks Iran — and it's looking increasingly likely that it will — Iran can be expected to kill many US soldiers with powerful attacks on the US military bases that are within striking range of its missiles. If that happens, the US can be expected to launch a full-scale regime change war on Iran.

If that's to be, then let this be the war that nobody comes to. Because the alternative is to fight and die in a stupid war waged by evil people, for nothing. •

We Must Oppose War With Iran At The Top Of Our Lungs

President Trump is reportedly returning to Washington early from a G7 summit in Canada and has told his national security council to prepare for an urgent meeting in the situation room, apparently to discuss Iran.

The US president has taken to social media to terrorize Iranian civilians, telling Tehran's millions of inhabitants that they must immediately evacuate the city and saying "Iran should have signed the 'deal' I told them to sign."

Weirdly, the strongest indication that Trump has made a decision to attack Iran might be a recent post on Truth Social about former Fox News darling Tucker Carlson.

"Somebody please explain to kooky Tucker Carlson that," IRAN CAN NOT HAVE A NUCLEAR WEAPON!" the president posted.

Carlson has been an outspoken critic of warmongering toward Iran, and was reportedly responsible for personally talking the president out of his Iran brinkmanship in the first Trump administration.

Antiwar's Scott Horton is reporting that, according to his sources, the Trump administration has already decided to join in Israel's war.

Capitol Hill is clearly worried that a war with Iran is imminent, with numerous lawmakers in the House and the Senate scrambling to get legislation in place that would stop the president from ordering such a war.

Benjamin Netanyahu has been speaking to the western press to argue in favor of assassinating Iran's Supreme Leader Ali Khamenei. I keep thinking about the Mad King in Game of Thrones who went nuts and kept ordering everyone to be burned, until a member of his own court decided enough is enough and slit his throat.

A full-scale US war against Iran is one of the worst things that could possibly happen. Full stop. It would likely entail millions of deaths, massive worldwide economic suffering, chaos and devastation throughout the middle east unlike anything we've ever seen, and could easily wind up with an Israeli nuclear weapon exploding in Tehran. There is a reason even a lot of otherwise war-happy swamp monsters in Washington have resisted going down this path. I really, really hope it doesn't happen.

If this is the direction the empire chooses to go, expect mass-scale psychological manipulation on an entirely unprecedented level to dupe the public into going along with this thing. Expect far more lies. Expect far more propaganda. Expect psyops. Maybe a false flag attack or two. It will be bad.

Don't buy into the lies. Oppose their warmongering at the top of your lungs, with everything you've got. I will be doing the same.

Anyone who supports this war is an enemy of the human species. ·

After Iraq There's No Excuse For Buying The War Lies About Iran
• Notes From The Edge Of The Narrative Matrix •

There is absolutely no excuse for buying into the war propaganda about Iran after what we all saw with Iraq.

"OMG nuclear weapons!" Shut up, idiot. If you're a grown adult with internet access still swallowing this load of bull spunk in the year 2025 you're either stupid or evil.

•

President Donald Trump is now saying he has no intention of seeking or facilitating a ceasefire with Iran, telling reporters that he's after a "complete give-up" from Iran instead.

"I'm not too much in a mood to negotiate," Trump said.

Asked by the press if he's worried about US troops being targeted by Iran in the coming days, the president said "We'll come down so hard if they do anything to our people. We'll come down so hard. The gloves are off. I think they know not to touch our troops."

This is a stupid, crazy lie. Iran has explicitly said it will strike US bases in the region if the US attacks Iranian territory. If you punch someone, you expect to be punched back.

If Trump orders US forces to bomb Iran, it will be because he wants to start a war and knowingly chose to do so.

•

One of the dumbest narratives we're currently being fed about Iran is the claim that Israel is precision-striking high-level targets in Iran while Iran is just bombing civilians all over the place in Israel.

A casual glance at the death tolls shows this is clearly false. As of this writing the current official death count sits at 24 Israelis killed by Iran and 224 Iranians killed by Israel — most of whom are reportedly civilians. On Friday they bombed a residential building and killed 60 people, including 20 kids.

•

Israeli Defense Minister Israel Katz thumped his chest on Twitter about an IDF strike on an Iranian television station on Monday, saying "The Iranian regime's propaganda and incitement broadcasting authority was attacked by the IDF after a widespread evacuation of residents in the area."

I wonder how the western press who are currently deceiving the public to promote Israel's information interests feel about this new rule that it's okay to bomb media outlets if someone decides they're propaganda?

•

People shouldn't be so hard on Trump about all this. You'd probably start a war with Iran too if someone was threatening to leak your child molestation video.

•

The war on Iran isn't really about nuclear weapons — if it was they would've kept the nuclear deal in place, which was working as intended. The Gaza holocaust isn't really about Hamas or hostages — if it was they would've just targeted Hamas or negotiated a hostage deal.

It's all lies. The war on Iran is about regional hegemony and the genocide in Gaza is about Israel's longstanding desire to remove all Palestinians from a Palestinian territory. It's not about self-defense, it's about land and power, and it always has been.

•

This is one of the reasons antiwar people have been focusing so hard on Gaza, by the way. It wasn't just because it's a horrific genocide happening right in front of us, it was because it always risked blowing up into a regional war involving Israel's western allies. We've been watching it expand into the West Bank, Lebanon, Yemen, Syria, and into Iran for a bit last year, and now it's blown up into all-out war between Israel and Iran with the US poised to join in.

For 20 months I've been getting people asking me why I've been so laser-focused on Gaza while paying less attention to this or that conflict or foreign policy issue. This is why. It's a waking nightmare in and of itself, but it's also always been a powderkeg that could explode into something much, much worse. •

Mike Huckabee Is A Deranged Armageddon Cultist
• Notes From The Edge Of The Narrative Matrix •

President Trump has shared a text message that was sent to him by Mike Huckabee, the deranged Christian Zionist who serves as the current US ambassador to Israel, and it is one of the creepiest things I have ever seen in my life.

The text reads as follows:

"Mr President,

God spared you in Butler, PA to be the most consequential President in a century — maybe ever. The decisions on your shoulders I would not want to be made by anyone else.

You have many voices speaking to you Sir, but there is only ONE voice that matters. HIS voice.

I am your appointed servant in this land and am available for you but I do not try to get in your presence often because I trust your instincts.

No President in my lifetime has been in a position like yours. Not since Truman in 1945. I don't reach out to persuade you. Only to encourage you.

I believe you will hear from heaven and that voice is far more important than mine or ANYONE else's.

You sent me to Israel to be your eyes, ears and voice and to make sure our flag flies above our embassy. My job is to be the last one to leave.

I will not abandon this post. Our flag will NOT come down! You did not seek this moment. This moment sought YOU!

It is my honor to serve you!

Mike Huckabee"

There are so many weird, creepy things about this message. The intensity. The religious fanaticism. The groveling, self-debasing obsequiousness, clearly designed to appeal to Trump's enormous ego. But by far the most disturbing part was the reference to Truman in 1945 — a nod to the last and only time a national leader used nuclear weapons against an enemy state.

Trump claims to have experienced a religious transformation after surviving an assassination attempt last year. Nuclear weapons and doomsday cultism are poor bedfellows. I really hope this is just some bizarre madman diplomacy and not an accurate reflection of something that is actually occurring inside the president's mind as he pushes toward direct confrontation with Iran.

•

The US and Israel don't oppose Iran getting nukes because they fear a nuclear attack by irrational tyrants, nor because they worry about Iran giving nukes to terrorist factions. They oppose Iran getting nukes because then all their regime change agendas go right out the window.

This isn't actually about nukes. It's about toppling Tehran so that the US and Israel can dominate the middle east. It's about regional hegemony and geostrategic control, and nothing else.

They'd be pushing for regime change in Iran whether they believed Iran was seeking a nuke or not.

•

How fucking stupid do you have to believe the lies about Iran? It's just a much dumber, much more obvious version of the Iraq war narratives, pushed by a much dumber, much more obvious US president. With the benefit of having watched it all happen before.

At least with the Iraq invasion Bush had a year and a half of soaring approval where he got to posture as the Good Guy protecting Americans from the Bad Guys. This time it's been a year and a half of the US backing history's first live-streamed genocide, with Israel essentially telling the world "WE'RE HITLER, WE'RE THE NEW NAZIS, WE KILL KIDS" for 20 months, and now they're getting ready to say that THIS is what US soldiers need to go fight and die for?

Come ON people. It's the same movie. They barely even changed the name, they just switched the Q to an N. There is no excuse for failing to see what's happening here.

•

A new Economist/YouGov poll found that only 19 percent of Americans currently support a US war with Iran. Most Americans oppose such a war, including a majority of Trump supporters.

People advocating regime change interventionism in Iran are arguing that the US needs to ignore the will of its own electorate in the name of spreading democracy.

•

There are no anti-war Trump supporters; if you're still supporting Trump, you're not anti-war. There are no anti-war Republicans; if you're still a member of the Republican Party, you're not anti-war. If you got scammed by Trump's anti-war schtick that's one thing, but it's another thing entirely if you're still buying into the scam after being taken by the hand and carefully shown that it's a scam in excruciating detail throughout Trump's second term.

If you supported Trump because you thought he was anti-war, the time is now to completely wash your hands of him and firmly take your stand against him. If you stood with the Republicans because you thought they were less warmongering than the Democrats, it's time to leave the party and join the actual anti-war movement. If you're not willing to do either of these things, it's time to stop pretending you don't love war.

•

I don't feel the same disdain toward people who got scammed by Trump's fake antiwar schtick that I see others expressing. I understand it, but I don't feel it. We live in an information ecosystem teeming with propaganda and deception, and people are going to get confused.

There's no shame in being deceived. There IS shame in deceiving. There IS shame in continuing to support a warmonger after you discover that you were deceived about him. But

BEING deceived in and of itself is no crime. That's why the perpetrator goes to jail in fraud cases and not the victims.

Mark Twain said "It's easier to fool people than to convince them that they have been fooled," and it's SO true. As social animals, humans are so dominated by the need to conform to our tribal loyalties that we've got psychological barriers to admitting that our tribe/faction got things wrong. And as social animals, shame is a powerful driving force in our psychological lives, because we're afraid of being seen as deficient by other humans.

But it's irrational for us to view those who are deceived as deficient, and it's irrational to feel shame about having gotten something wrong. I've gotten lots of things wrong over the years. I'm sure there are some things I'm still getting wrong. Being willing to see you got it wrong is the essential first step to getting it right. Always being open to the possibility that you could be wrong is necessary to forming a truth-based relationship with reality.

If you were duped by the MAGA scam, that's okay. Just take what you learned and start working on re-orienting yourself toward truth. You know what's false, so now you can start working on finding out what's true. And you can start constructing a new worldview accordingly. •

Bombing Hospitals Is Bad Again
• Notes From The Edge Of The Narrative Matrix •

Israel and its western allies are crying and rending their garments about an Israeli hospital that was damaged in an Iranian missile strike. Western media outlets like the BBC and New York Times have suddenly remembered how to write headlines which assign blame to the attacker after deciding that hospitals getting bombed is a newsworthy event again.

The Iranian attack didn't even kill anybody, and the damage to the hospital was reportedly the result of a shockwave from a strike on a nearby Israeli military facility. That's right: the Israeli military was using the hospital for human shields. As always, every accusation is a confession.

Israel, as we all know, bombs hospitals constantly. Israel bombed an Iranian hospital just the other day to almost no coverage from the western press. Israel has attacked healthcare workers and healthcare facilities in Gaza around 700 times according to the World Health Organisation, and the IDF has repeatedly been documented entering the hospitals it attacks to destroy individual pieces of medical equipment. Israel, unlike Iran, is deliberately targeting healthcare facilities to make Gaza unlivable.

Israeli defense minister Israel Katz is now saying that because of the hospital strike, Iranian Ayatollah Ali Khamenei "cannot continue to exist." Knowing what we know about Israel's track record, saying that people who bomb hospitals should not be allowed to exist can only be interpreted as an extremely antisemitic statement.

•

The only way the US wins a war with Iran easily, quickly, and without massive losses is if it uses a nuclear weapon. This fact, combined with that Huckabee post comparing Trump to Truman in 1945 and Trump's "evacuate Tehran" and "UNCONDITIONAL SURRENDER" statements, makes me nervous.

And the Americans are reportedly discussing using nuclear weapons on Iran already. Fox News reports that the Trump administration has not ruled out any options regarding the possibility of using a tactical nuke to destroy an Iranian nuclear facility.

That's right kids, we've got to nuke the Iranians to liberate the Iranians. We've got to stop Iran from obtaining nuclear weapons because a nuclear-armed despotic regime might use those powerful weapons to do crazy and reckless things, like drop a tactical nuke on a foreign nation's power plant.

•

Israel: [Massacres children, bombs hospitals, assassinates journalists, starves civilians, kills aid workers, murders starving civilians seeking aid, destroys Gaza, assaults the West Bank, invades Syria, invades Lebanon, bombs Yemen, bombs Iran]

Iran: [Bombs Israel back]

World: Hooray!

Israel [crying]: They hate us because of our religion!

•

I've never understood why people think "you hate Israel!" is an insult. If you knew a guy who was constantly murdering children and setting fire to his neighbors' homes while meddling in your home life, you'd probably hate that guy. The problem is people don't hate Israel enough.

•

If you've never been called an antisemite then you are way too chill about genocide.

•

If your case for going to war contains the words "the Bible says" or "God commands us", then you do not have a case for going to war.

•

Tucker Carlson conducted a two-hour interview with Senator Ted Cruz in which he aggressively interrogated the lawmaker's hawkish position on Iran. There are a lot of clips from the interview going around online, the most famous of which features Carlson asking Cruz basic questions about Iran's population which the Texas senator is unable to answer.

The lesson here isn't that war hawks are too lazy or stupid to learn things about the nations they want to destroy, the lesson is that they are lying when they say they care about the people in those nations and want to liberate them.

They don't care about Iranian people. At all. They care about power, empire-building, oil, and Israel, and then they make up a bunch of stories about wanting to rescue the people they're about to murder from the rule of a tyrannical regime.

All wars are built on lies. •

War Is The Worst Thing In The World

War is the worst thing in the world. It is the single craziest behavior exhibited by humans. The most destructive. The most traumatizing. The least sustainable. The least conducive to human thriving.

All the things we fear most become the norm in a land ravaged by war. Death. Pain. Suffering. Rape. Chaos. Uncertainty. Losing loved ones. Losing homes. Losing limbs. Living in terror. Being attacked. Being brain damaged. Being faced with impossible choices. All the things we frighten ourselves with by watching horror movies become a reality from which there is no escape.

War creates a waking nightmare which any sensible person would want to avoid except in the direst necessity. And yet we are ruled by people who actively seek it out. Who will lie and manipulate to make wars happen. Who will smear and slander anyone who resists in the name of peace. Who will actively fight against every healthy impulse in everybody in their society to push their war agenda forward.

They always tell us the new war they want us to fight is about self-defense, or about liberating an oppressed population from a tyrannical dictatorship, or about preventing terrorism, or about spreading freedom and democracy. Usually they tell us it's about all of these things.

But it never is. They are always lying. Always. They are pushing human beings into the worst circumstances they could possibly experience here on earth for no other reason than power and profit. To advance the hegemonic agendas of empire managers and to fill the coffers of war profiteers. That's all it ever is. Always, always, always.

They say whatever they need to say and move whatever chess pieces they need to move to get their war, and then they send a bunch of poor suckers to go fight in it, lying to them that they are doing something noble and heroic.

They ship them off to a foreign land, and then they are trapped. They can't flee into the wilderness because they don't know how to survive and have no way of getting home. They can't ask the locals for help because the locals are their victims. They have no choice but to either fight and kill people who have never wronged them, or lay down their arms and be caged like animals.

If they choose to fight, the best case scenario is that they spend the rest of their lives knowing that they killed other human beings who wanted to live just as much as themselves, and who had just as much right to. All because some people who already had far too much power wanted a little bit more.

It's about the most insane and backwards thing you could possibly imagine. The most powerful individuals in our world are people who actively push for the absolute worst outcomes that could possibly happen. It's the exact opposite of the way things should be.

Yet we are told it's normal. We are trained to believe this is just the reality we live in which we should expect and accept, first by our parents and teachers, and then by our news media and by Hollywood. War is aggressively normalized by pundits, propagandists and politicians, and enthusiastically glorified in movies and documentaries.

Those who were forced or duped into fighting in these insane arrangements of mass-scale violence are framed as heroes, and anyone who disagrees with what they were sent to do is framed as disrespectful and ungrateful. Those who push for peace are framed as treasonous freaks who must surely have covert loyalties toward whatever government the empire is trying to target this time around. Those who suggest that there might be some solution apart from war are dismissed as infantile dreamers.

And once the war has started, it is almost impossible to stop. The entire political/media class treats the war as the new normal, and any suggestion that it's time to wrap things up is regarded as outlandish and suspicious. It's never time to end the war, because this or that objective has not yet been achieved, or because this or that faction might come into power if troops are pulled out, or because this or that disempowered group might suffer without our military there to protect them.

Ending a war is as difficult as beginning a war is easy. All the institutions which lined up perfectly to help get the ball rolling toward war suddenly transform into giant tar pits of inertia when it comes to ending the conflict. The warmakers say the war must continue for this or that reason, the politicians back the warmakers, the media back the politicians, and the person saying it's time to end the madness is left standing there looking like they're the crazy ones.

But they're not the crazy ones. The ones pushing us toward war are crazy. This whole system is crazy. This whole civilization.

The ones resisting the push toward war are the ones fighting for sanity. They're the ones who are trying to reverse the tide of madness and drag us into a healthy world.

If this is you, do not falter. Do not let the warmongers shout you down or shut you up. You are right, and they are wrong. Let your voice thunder with confidence. Let nothing cause you to waver.

Blessed are the peacemakers. Don't let anyone trick you into doubting what you know to be true. •

Tulsi Gabbard Is A Warmongering Asshole

President Trump has twice thrown his own intelligence chief Tulsi Gabbard under the bus, repeatedly telling the press that the national intelligence director was wrong when she told Congress in March that the American spy network does not believe Iran is attempting to obtain a nuclear weapon.

To be clear, when Gabbard made this statement she was not voicing her personal opinion, she was repeating verbatim the findings laid out in the 2025 Threat Assessment of the intelligence agencies of the United States, which said "We continue to assess Iran is not building a nuclear weapon and that Khamenei has not reauthorized the nuclear weapons program he suspended in 2003, though pressure has probably built on him to do so."

Despite this, Trump has been publicly expressing disdain for his intelligence director, flatly saying "she's wrong" when asked about Gabbard's testimony on Friday, and saying "I don't care what she says" when asked the same question about Gabbard's statement earlier this week.

Rather than push back on the president's crude dismissal, Gabbard took to social media to tell everyone that Trump is actually right about Iran, and that everyone who thought she said Iran isn't seeking a nuclear weapon is imagining things.

"The dishonest media is intentionally taking my testimony out of context and spreading fake news as a way to manufacture division," Gabbard said on Twitter. "America has intelligence that Iran is at the point that it can produce a nuclear weapon within weeks to months, if they decide to finalize the assembly. President Trump has been clear that can't happen, and I agree. My full testimony below:"

Bizarrely, Gabbard accompanied this text with a video clip of her congressional testimony in March which in no way validates anything she says in her post. Nowhere in the clip does she utter anything about Iran being weeks to months from a nuclear weapon, and she explicitly says the words "the IC [Intelligence Community] continues to assess Iran is not building a nuclear weapon and the Iranian Supreme Leader Khamenei has not authorized a nuclear weapons program that he suspended in 2003."

A recent report from CNN says that according to US intelligence sources Iran is not "weeks to months" from a nuclear weapon but years, reporting that Tehran is "up to three years away from being able to produce and deliver one to a target of its choosing."

This kind of post-truth society behavior, where one tells people they're not seeing what's directly in front of their eyes, is the kind of thing you only expect from Donald Trump and his most obsequious bootlickers. And what we are witnessing here is Tulsi Gabbard getting down on her knees and putting tongue to leather.

Tulsi Gabbard is a warmongering asshole, and a liar. She is helping to deceive the world into yet another horrible middle eastern war, and if she and her fellow warmongers succeed her words will go down in history as among the most depraved lies ever told.

This is the same person who tweeted back in March, "President Trump IS the President of Peace. He is ending bloodshed across the world and will deliver lasting peace in the Middle East."

This is also the person who attacked Trump's hawkishness on Iran constantly while campaigning for president as a Democrat in the 2020 primary race.

"Intel officials & politicians led us into Iraq war," Gabbard tweeted in 2019. "Now Trump's using the same playbook to lead our country into war with Iran. The cost in lives & treasure will be infinitely greater than the wars in Iraq, Afghanistan, & Syria, and will undermine our ntnl security."

"The main responsibility of the president is to keep Americans safe. Trump has failed — undermining our national security by tearing up the Iran nuclear deal, threatening military action, bringing us closer to war with

Iran that will be far worse than war in Iraq," reads another 2019 tweet.

"They are setting the stage for a war with Iran that would prove to be far more costly, far more devastating and dangerous than anything that we saw in the Iraq War," Gabbard said of the Trump administration during a 2019 interview on ABC.

This fraudster has built an entire political career out of pretending to oppose war and militarism in order to win the support of Americans who are sick of pouring blood and treasure into the US slaughter machine, opportunistically drifting to whatever corner of the political spectrum would offer her the most power, and then when she got as high as she can go she sold all her stated principles to the furthest extent possible at the earliest opportunity.

Pee fetish porn stars have more dignity and integrity.

I feel so stupid for having bought into Gabbard's antiwar schtick early on. Fuck this asshole, fuck Trump, fuck Israel, and fuck the US empire. •

Israel Supporters Will Be Despised For The Rest of Their Lives
• Notes From The Edge Of The Narrative Matrix •

Do Israel's supporters know it's over for them? Like, they know they're going to be despised for the rest of their lives, right? That they will never, ever live down the fact that they supported a live-streamed genocide? And that it will only get worse for them as history clarifies things?

Surely they must realize this by now. Surely they must realize that nothing they do for the rest of their lives will ever be as significant as the fact that they played cheerleader for genocide and all of Israel's demented warmongering, long after normal people realized it was the wrong thing to do. That in the eyes of the world they will all always be first and foremost someone who supported and defended history's first live-streamed genocide.

I wonder what that's like, knowing that about yourself? If that was me maybe I'd be pushing for World War Three as well, I dunno. Maybe I'd hope we could turn the whole world into Gaza and let the flames wash away human memory of the things we had done. That enough death and destruction spread out across enough of the earth would make my crimes look small in comparison or something.

It won't work, though. Everyone's always going to remember what they did. Their grandchildren will be disgusted by them. Their families will carry their shame for generations.

What a terrible way to be.

•

The UK will reportedly be designating Palestine Action as a terrorist group for spraying British military planes with red paint to protest the genocide in Gaza.

It says a lot about how backwards and diseased western civilization has become when peace activists are designated as terrorists for trying to stop the world's worst acts of terrorism.

•

Iran is having more and more success with its missile strikes on Israel. I am not a military expert, but I've been hearing for years that Israel doesn't want to fight Iran because it can't reliably stop Iran's missiles. Israel of course would have known this, so it looks like the plan was always for Israel to get itself into hot water and have the US pull it out.

•

Iran's real sin is insisting upon its own sovereignty as a nation. That's why it's a target of the western empire. Giving up sovereignty over its own energy infrastructure would be giving up the very thing the Iranians started fighting for in the first place all those years ago. They're not going to do it unless they are forced to, otherwise what was the point of resisting absorption into the imperial blob that whole time?

•

I'm supposed to hate a country for saying "Death to America"? I yell that during sex.

•

The only reason they get to call the Gaza holocaust a "war" is because they're using bombs and bullets to do the extermination. If they were using gas chambers to kill the same number of people with the exact same motive, all it would change is the world's understanding of what's happening.

•

War after war after war the western empire has told us it needs to ship off our young to go fight evil murderous tyrants, only for the west to wake up to the reality that the empire's dearest ally in the middle east is the most evil, murderous and tyrannical regime around.

•

The idea of war with Iran would be even less popular than it is now if the western media hadn't spent all these years referring to Iran's civilian nuclear energy program as "Iran's nuclear program", deliberately causing people to assume that Iran is working on nuclear weapons.

•

Friendly reminder that last year the official Democratic Party platform slammed Trump for choosing not to go to war with Iran in 2018, 2019 and 2020 during his last presidency.

Americans aren't allowed to vote against war. •

Trump Has Bombed Iran. What Happens Next Is His Fault.

The US military has bombed multiple Iranian nuclear sites on the orders of President Trump, immediately putting tens of thousands of US military personnel in the region at risk of an Iranian retaliation which can then escalate to full-scale war.

Earlier this month Iran's Defense Minister Aziz Nasirzadeh explicitly warned the United States that a direct US attack would result in Tehran ordering strikes on US bases in the middle east, saying "all US bases are within our reach and we will boldly target them in host countries."

In the lead-up to Trump's act of war on Iran, the president told the press that an attack on American troops will mean a harsh response from the US, saying, "We'll come down so hard if they do anything to our people. We'll come down so hard. The gloves are off. I think they know not to touch our troops."

Trump reiterated this threat to Iran in his announcement of the US attack today.

"There will be either peace, or there will be tragedy for Iran, far greater than we have witnessed over the last eight days," Trump said. "Remember, there are many targets left. Tonight's was the most difficult of them all, by far, and perhaps the most lethal. But if peace does not come quickly,

we will go after those other targets with precision, speed and skill. Most of them can be taken out in a matter of minutes."

So you can see how we might already be on our way toward a war of nightmarish proportions as a result of the president's unprovoked act of aggression. Tehran now has to choose between reestablishing deterrence with extreme aggression or opening the floodgates to a whole host of existential threats from both outside and inside the country. Add to that the possibility of Iran blockading the Strait of Hormuz and the fact that Iran has now been strongly incentivized to actually obtain a nuclear weapon, and it looks very likely that we are plunging into a situation that could unfold in any number of horrific ways.

Right now American political discourse is rife with the narrative that the US has been "dragged" into Israel's war, which I reject entirely. Every step of the way this entire thing has been signed off on by US leadership. We are at this point because Trump and his regime knowingly chose to take us here.

US troops within reach of Iran's missiles are reportedly being briefed that they can expect to be on the receiving end of retaliatory strikes in the coming days.

Again, Iran **explicitly** warned it would attack the US military if the US military did the thing it just did. If and when these retaliatory strikes come, the warmongers will try to argue that

this is a valid reason to escalate this war. They will be lying. They chose to make this happen.

Whatever transpires from this point on is the fault of Donald Trump and the unelected thugs he listens to. If US troops are killed, the war sluts in Washington and the Pentagon propagandists in the press will list their names and bandy about their photos and demand that their deaths be avenged with further acts of war — but it will not be Iran's fault that they died.

It will be Trump's fault. It will be the fault of everyone whose decisions led up to bombs being dropped on Iranian energy infrastructure, and the fault of everyone who put those soldiers in harm's way.

None of this needed to happen. Iran was at the negotiating table. The Iran deal was working fine before Trump shredded it to put us on this terrible trajectory. The warmongers artificially manufactured this situation and knowingly inflicted this horror upon our world.

I am really not looking forward to all the melodramatic victim-LARPing if and when Iran kills US military personnel stationed in west Asia. The US is the only nation on earth that can rival Israel in its ability to play the victim when the ball they've thrown at the wall bounces back.

US State Department Spokeswoman Says Israel Is Greater Than America

• Notes From The Edge Of The Narrative Matrix •

Journalist Ken Klippenstein has drawn attention to an overlooked remark made by State Department spokeswoman Tammy Bruce last month saying that the United States is "the greatest country on earth, next to Israel."

"The pride of being able to be here and do work that facilitates making things better for people and in the greatest country on Earth, next to Israel," Bruce told Jewish News Syndicate. "It's an honor to be able to make a difference and to be able to speak in this regard with an administration that I love so much and that I feel genuinely represented by."

It's like this administration is doing everything it can to vindicate those who accuse it of being Israel First instead of America First.

•

I feel like we don't talk enough about the fact that Donald Trump publicly admitted to being bought and owned by the richest Israeli on earth, Republican megadonor Miriam Adelson.

On the campaign trail last year Trump told the Israeli American Council Summit that the first time he was president, Miriam and her late husband Sheldon "would come into the White House probably almost more than anybody, outside of people that work there." He said they were always after something, "always for Israel," and "as soon as I'd give them something, they'd want something else." He named the US recognition of the occupied Golan Heights as part of Israel as one of the gifts he showered the Zionist state with to please the Adelsons, who pumped hundreds of millions of dollars into his presidential campaigns.

•

It's hard to focus on Israel's airstrikes in Lebanon due to Israel's invasion of Syria, which is hard to focus on due to Israel's atrocities in the West Bank, which are hard to focus on due to Israel's genocide in Gaza, which is hard to focus on due to Israel's war on Iran, which is hard to focus on because of America's war on Iran.

•

Top Ten dumbest things we're being asked to believe about Iran:

1. That the Iranians want to be bombed.

2. That the guy bombing Iran wants peace.

3. That regime change interventionism is a swell idea this time.

4. That anyone who doesn't want war with Iran hates Jews.

5. That this time the government and the media are telling us the truth about an American war.

6. That this time the neocons are smart and correct.

7. That bombing Iran makes it LESS likely to try to obtain nukes.

8. That Iran is trying to assassinate the US president when all US presidents have the same foreign policy.

9. That Iran (a country that never starts wars) cannot be trusted with nuclear weapons, but Israel (a country that starts wars constantly) can.

10. That attacking Iran benefits Americans.

•

It blows my mind that there are people trying to argue that Trump does not seek war. What do these idiots think the United States would do if another country started bombing American energy infrastructure?

•

I'm trying to get an important business deal done, so I firebombed the guy's house to make him more likely to negotiate with me. I just want peace.

•

The following things are antisemitic:

- opposing war with Iran

- viewing Palestinians as human

- opposing genocide

- Greta Thunberg

- peace

- journalism

- Ms Rachel

- truth

- critical thinking

- the UN

- Tucker Carlson

- Amnesty International

- Human Rights Watch

- equal rights

•

It's hilarious that anyone still takes this "antisemitism" schtick seriously. Oh no there's a special group of white people who might get hurt feelings if I don't want to send my kids to invade Iran.

•

The western world has been on a two-year crash course learning all the reasons why the Muslim world has been correct about Israel this entire time.

•

It's kind of nice to be arguing with George W Bush conservatives about US foreign policy again. For the last few years I've been getting called a Nazi by western Zionists and a Putin-loving fascist by NATO simps; it's refreshing to be hated for the hippie moonbat I actually am for once. •

Iran Shows Us Why The US And Israel Should Not Be Allowed To Have Nukes

Well it's been a crazy couple of days.

Trump bombed Iran's civilian nuclear energy facilities in an attack that CNN reports did no lasting damage, and Iran exercised extraordinary restraint with symbolic retaliatory strikes on US military bases coordinated to avoid American casualties — a move many are comparing to Iran's non-lethal response to the US assassination of General Qassem Soleimani in 2020.

After pumping out deception and fake diplomacy for weeks in order to assist Israel's unprovoked war on Iran and launch an unprovoked attack on his own, Trump took to social media to proudly celebrate his administration's facilitation of a ceasefire to the war he himself needlessly started, like an arsonist giving himself a trophy for extinguishing one of his own house fires.

And, for the moment at least, the ceasefire appears to be holding. Which is good. There are a lot of terrible people who did everything they could to get Iran to kill US troops and spark a horrific war, but Iran didn't take the bait. Iran doesn't want war at all. Trump found out that Americans disapproved of the airstrikes and opposed war with Iran. And Israel found out that fighting an actual military force is a lot less easy than fighting hospital patients and children.

So for now we've got a ceasefire.

We have never been shown any evidence that Iran was working on obtaining nuclear weapons, which given the US empire's extensive history of lying about this sort of thing means we should assume it was not. But it has certainly been given every incentive to obtain them now, given that that's probably the only thing that can stop the US and Israel from casually committing these egregious acts of aggression whenever they feel like it.

And isn't it interesting how Iran keeps demonstrating a degree of restraint that we all know we'd never see from the United States or Israel if another country bombed their energy infrastructure or assassinated their military leaders, and yet Iran is the country we're told can never be trusted with nuclear weapons?

The US empire and Israel both exist in a perpetual state of war and attack other countries constantly; Iran never invades other countries and avoids war like Melania Trump avoids missionary position. But we're meant to accept that it's fine for the US and Israel to have nukes and do anything necessary to prevent Iran from getting any?

Even if you accept the evidence-free premise that Iran would do crazy and reckless things if it became a nuclear-armed state, there is no rational argument that Trump and his handlers have been going about preventing this outcome intelligently. As Joe Lauria explains

in Consortium News, the Iran nuclear deal was a remarkable achievement of international diplomacy that was working fine until Trump shredded it in 2018. Iran was following all the agreed upon rules and its nuclear enrichment was capped at 3.67 percent, but Trump killed it because the Zionists and warmongers who brought him to power want more aggression toward Iran instead of less.

It's so intensely stupid that we have to keep doing this horrifying dance every few years just because there are too many war-horny freaks with way too much power inside the US empire. And every time they get closer to getting their wish. Iran is being given more and more reasons to view the US and Israel as an existential threat, more and more motive to obtain nuclear weapons, and less and less reason to negotiate anything with Washington.

These bastards keep pushing us toward something very ugly. Let's hope people keep waking up to the depravity of Israel and the US empire before the warmakers succeed in obtaining their long-sought prize. •

Dear Israel Apologist

Dear Israel apologist,

There is nothing you can say to me that will make me stop opposing Israel's western-backed atrocities.

Call me an antisemite or a Nazi or any name you want. The name-calling stopped having any effect a long time ago.

Babble about October 7 and Hamas and hostages all you wish. I've stopped listening to you.

Pile on as many walls of text as you like explaining why it is actually fine and good to bomb hospitals and massacre starving civilians seeking aid. I ain't reading all that, free Palestine.

Regurgitate whatever the latest propaganda narrative is about Iran or the Houthis or Hezbollah or whichever new war Israel is getting ready to start this week. We both know it's all lies.

Parrot whatever's the current hasbara slogan justifying Israel's genocide in Gaza if you want to. Your words have no power here.

That's why your old tricks have stopped working, you know: all you have is words.

We have truth, facts and morality on our side, and you have a bunch of words.

We have mountains of raw video footage documenting war crimes and mass atrocities. And you have a mountain of words.

We have an unshakable confidence in our opposition to history's first live-streamed genocide, and you have a river of verbiage.

Your weapons don't work here. This is not a fair fight. You are as outmatched as the helpless children being slaughtered by the Israeli military.

I am going to keep opposing the crimes of Israel and the western sponsors of its atrocities.

I am going to keep opposing the wars that Israel and its western backers are always starting in the middle east.

I am going to keep opposing the US empire which is fueled by human blood.

I am going to keep opposing the western media who spread war propaganda and normalize genocide.

I am going to keep opposing all the systems, institutions and ideologies which have given rise to the Gaza holocaust.

I am going to keep mocking your manipulations and weakening the power of your words.

There is nothing you can say to stop me from doing this.

There is nothing you can say to stop anyone from doing this.

Because all you have is words.

And nobody's listening anymore. •

The Fictional Mental Illness That Only Affects Enemies Of The Western Empire

Within the storytelling of western politics and punditry there exists a fictional type of mental illness which only affects people the US empire doesn't like.

If Iran gets a nuclear weapon, its crazy lunatic government will flip out and nuke us all.

Watch out for Hamas, Hezbollah and the Houthis, those guys are a bunch of maniacal antisemites who want to attack Israelis just because they're Jewish.

Oh no, Putin is invading Ukraine completely unprovoked because he's a madman who hates freedom and won't stop until he's conquered all of Europe.

China is building up its military because the megalomaniacal Xi Jinping wants to take over the world; all those US military bases surrounding China are just a defensive measure to contain Beijing's insanity.

Assad just went nuts one day and started slaughtering his own people out of nowhere.

Gaddafi is a sexual sadist who's giving Viagra to his troops to help them commit mass rapes in Libya.

Saddam Hussein is so crazy and evil he's trying to obtain weapons of mass destruction to give Americans another 9/11.

The North Koreans used to be far too insane to be allowed to have nuclear weapons because they'd nuke San Francisco immediately, but after they obtained nuclear weapons they were miraculously cured of this rare psychological disorder.

The stories of the western empire ask us to believe that everyone who finds themselves in the imperial crosshairs is an irrational actor whose loony behavior can only be attributed to some uncontrollable defect within their own minds, or who will soon snap and do something nutty if they are not contained by force.

One antagonist who never appears in these fairy tales of the western empire is the western empire itself. In the storytelling of the empire, there is no globe-spanning power structure which is constantly inflicting violence and destruction upon populations around the world while seeking to crush any nation who disobeys its dictates. It's just a bunch of irrational psychos, seeking nuclear weapons and becoming aggressively militaristic for no other reason than because they are crazy, while the totally normal alliance led by a totally normal country in North America innocently responds to their crazy behavior.

That's the story. In real life, the most aggressive and unreasonable actor on the world stage by far is the empire-like power structure that is loosely centralized around Washington DC. Nobody else is constantly waging wars of aggression around the world.

Nobody else is circling the planet with hundreds of military bases for the purpose of global domination. Nobody else has spent the 21st century killing millions of people and deliberately targeting civilians with starvation sanctions in countries on the other side of the planet. Only the US-centralized empire has been doing these things.

But we are asked to believe that this vicious imperial power structure is the only rational actor on earth, and that those who resist its aggressions are the crazy ones.

And you are told that if you can't see this, then you're crazy too. You're a crackpot. A conspiracy theorist. A paranoid nutball whose voice should be marginalized and whose ideas should be dismissed with a scoff.

You are crazy if you don't believe what the world's craziest power structure says about its enemies being crazy.

It is gaslighting on a global scale. It is madness, and that is why this civilization has gone mad.

Let's hope someone finds a way to protect the world from the insanity of the western empire. •

Uh–Oh! Political Antisemitism Smears Have Stopped Working!
• Notes From The Edge Of The Narrative Matrix •

Israel supporters everywhere have been in full blown crisis mode for days because, apparently, antisemitism smears have stopped working.

Zohran Mamdani has won the Democratic Party primary in the New York City mayoral race after a frenetic smear campaign to portray him as an antisemite for his pro-Palestinian views, and now all the world's worst people are freaking out about it.

I'm seeing some intensely rabid Islamophobia throughout public discourse in response to Mamdani's win, the likes of which I haven't seen since 9/11. All this hatred we're now seeing directed toward Muslims is going to look pretty weird after the imperial crosshairs shift to Beijing and all these same people start acting super duper concerned about the plight of Muslims in Xinjiang.

I never get excited about anything that happens in the Democratic Party anymore, but the fact that these smears have lost a lot of their power has some encouraging and far-reaching implications for western politics in general. Things have come a long way since the psyop against Jeremy Corbyn.

•

The British government has "strongly condemned" a live performance on the BBC by rap duo Bob Vylan in which the crowd was led through a chant of "Death, death to the IDF." British police are investigating the incident as a potential criminal offense, and Zionists everywhere are treating this incident like a second Holocaust.

Inside the western empire it's considered offensive and unacceptable to say "death to" a foreign military comprised entirely of armed combatants which is presently committing a genocide in full view of the entire world. It is not, however considered offensive and unacceptable to commit genocide.

So, just to be clear —

SAYING "death to" the foreign military which is presently committing genocide: wrong, unacceptable, outrageous, no.

CAUSING death to a civilian population because of their ethnicity by that same foreign military force: fine, normal, absolutely, yes.

•

Israeli is not a religion and Jewish is not a nationality and anti-Zionism is not anti-semitism and all decent people despise the state of Israel.

•

Hating Israel is one of the most patriotic things Americans can do at this point. It's clear now that Israel is going to keep aggressively pushing for a US war against Iran until they get it, and making support for Israel politically toxic in the US may be the only thing that can prevent them from succeeding.

•

I don't like the far right OR the far left. I like things to stay in the moderate center, where genocide is fine and people's healthcare money is given to cruise missile manufacturers.

•

They're not going to let any journalists into Gaza until the whole thing's been emptied out and they've hidden all the evidence of their holocaust — and then they'll call you an antisemitic conspiracy theorist if you say it happened.

•

I've never understood the debate about whether or not support for Israel is commanded in the Bible. If you think the Bible commands you to support what's being done in Gaza, then throw your Bible in the trash and get a different religion, because it's plainly false and immoral.

It is not legitimate to offload your responsibility for your own behavior onto your religion. If your religion commanded you to sexually molest children, it would be your moral responsibility as a human being to disobey your religion and stop following it. Gaza's no different.

•

A charismatic pro-Palestinian Muslim becoming the Democratic nominee for mayor of New York City. Westerners chanting "death to the IDF" and having a great time doing it. Israeli soldiers confessing their genocidal atrocities in the Israeli press. Israel's PR stranglehold is finally ending. •

Practice Small, Daily Acts Of Sabotage Against The Imperial Machine
• Notes From The Edge Of The Narrative Matrix •

Do something every day to help undermine public perception of the empire.

Draw attention to its abuses in places like Gaza.

Get people laughing at its absurdities and hypocrisies.

Spread distrust in the imperial propaganda services known as the western press by spotlighting their deceptions and manipulations.

Help people to recognize all the ways their government is screwing them over for the benefit of the rich and powerful.

Facilitate the collective dawning of the realization that everything westerners have been taught about their society and their world is a lie.

Help people to understand that it really, truly does not need to be this way.

Use every means at your disposal to help open up the next pair of eyelids to the ugly reality of the empire.

Cultivate a habit of daily acts of sabotage against the imperial machine. There is always something you can do.

You cannot defeat the machine by yourself, but you can do something every day to help tilt our society's collective consciousness toward tearing it down together.

I still can't get over how we're being asked to pretend "Death, death to the IDF" is some kind of hate crime at the exact same time IDF soldiers are telling the Israeli press they're being ordered to massacre starving civilians at aid sites.

I've been seeing a number of people arguing that it's wrong to say "death to the IDF" because soldiers aren't to be blamed for the criminality of their government. This framing is only accepted in the west because western soldiers also do evil things that our society needs to make up excuses for.

As an aside, "Death, death to the IDF" is an insanely catchy earworm. Been dancing around in my mind all day.

•

Deliberately starving a civilian population and then setting up aid sites as a death trap to massacre starving people trying to get food is too evil to wrap your mind around. If we saw a supervillain doing this in a movie we'd think it was dumb, because it wouldn't be believable.

•

•

It's like everyone's standing around watching a man beat a small child to death at a restaurant.

"Should we do something?" someone asks.

"You saw the kid throw food at the guy," someone replies. "The man has a right to defend himself."

"But he's killing him!"

"It's a fight. Bad things happen in a fight."

"Yeah, the boy shouldn't have started a fight he can't win."

"You're actually being quite hateful right now."

And sure, maybe it's true the child did set the man off by throwing food at him.

Maybe the child did so fully knowing that it would send the man into a murderous rage, because the man had been horrifically abusing the child his entire life.

Maybe instigating a physical confrontation in full view of the public was the child's last desperate attempt to expose the man's depravity, in the hope that everyone would finally see what's happening and do something to stop the abuse.

But nobody's stopping it, because the man has spent years charming and befriending everyone in town — or frightening and intimidating them if that's easier.

So now everyone's watching a grown man beat a child to death and pretending they're watching a fight, when they all know deep down what they're really watching is a cold-blooded murder by a cold-hearted man, who should have been stopped and locked away a long time ago.

•

The head of the International Atomic Energy Agency is saying that Iran could probably start enriching uranium again within a few months, which Iran has said it plans to do, and which Trump has said will result in another US bombing assault.

Trumpers tried to argue that the bombing of Iran was a brilliant strategic maneuver to avoid full-scale war, when it appears to have only made such a war much more likely. Now the president is saying he'll bomb Iran again if it resumes enriching uranium, something it will probably be able to do quite soon, after giving Iran every reason to start actively seeking a nuclear weapon.

When Iran hawks were arguing against the JCPOA (the Iran nuclear deal laid out during the Obama administration), one of their most common talking points was that it was "kicking the can down the road" to a nuclear-armed Iran in the future. In reality the JCPOA was a remarkable feat of international diplomacy that could have avoided all these needless escalations, and it is Trump and the Iran hawks who have been kicking the can down the road to full-scale war with Iran (if Iran doesn't get nukes first).

There's a lot to despise Trump for, but spending both of his terms setting the US on a trajectory toward war with Iran ranks right up around the top of the list. The JCPOA was working fine, but Trump shredded it in 2018 to set us on this path that is only getting darker and darker at a faster and faster pace. Trump chose that course of action to implement his "maximum pressure campaign" on Iran. Trump chose to assassinate Soleimani. Trump chose to bomb Iran. Everything that happens from here on out is Trump's fault. •

The Trumpanyahu Administration

Honestly at this point they should just get Netanyahu his own room in the White House and a desk in the Oval Office.

The prime minister of Israel is taking his third trip to the White House in the five months since Trump has been back in office. I have immediate blood family members who I love with all my heart and visit less often than this.

This comes as the Trump administration revokes the US visas of British punk rap duo Bob Vylan ahead of a US tour for chanting "Death, death to the IDF" at a concert in the UK. Trump's sycophantic supporters who spent years complaining that their free speech rights were under assault appear fine with their government deciding what words Americans are allowed to hear in their own country.

This also comes as Trump actively intervenes in the Israeli judicial system to prevent Netanyahu's corruption trial from moving forward.

The president has repeatedly taken to social media to demand that Israel abandon its corruption case against the prime minister, at one point even implying that the US could cut off arms supplies if his trial isn't canceled.

"The United States of America spends Billions of Dollar a year, far more than on any other Nation, protecting and supporting Israel," Trump said. "We are not going to stand for this. We just had a Great Victory with Prime Minister Bibi Netanyahu at the helm — And this greatly tarnishes our Victory. LET BIBI GO, HE'S GOT A BIG JOB TO DO!"

It's so revealing what the US government is and is not willing to threaten conditioning military supplies on, and what it's willing to interfere in Israel's affairs to accomplish.

Ever since the Gaza holocaust began we've been hearing lines like "Israel is a sovereign country" and "Israel is a sovereign state that makes its own decisions" when reporters ask why the White House doesn't leverage arms shipments to demand more humanitarian treatment for civilians in the Gaza Strip. But the president of the United States is willing to leverage those same arms shipments to directly interfere in Israeli legal proceedings which have nothing to do with the US government in order to get Netanyahu out of trouble.

And it would appear that the president's intervention has been successful; Netanyahu's corruption trial has since been postponed.

When it comes to committing genocide using American weapons funded by American taxpayers, Israel is a sovereign state upon which the US can exert zero leverage or control. When it comes to meddling in the corruption trial of a man who is wanted for war crimes by the International Criminal Court, the White House pulls no punches in protecting its favorite genocide monster.

There is no meaningful separation between the US and Israeli governments. They're two member states in the undeclared empire that sprawls across the entire western world, and Trump and Netanyahu are two of the most depraved and most consequential managers of this empire today.

They are thick as thieves. They are partners in crime.

Call it the Trumpanyahu administration. •

Israel Supporters Are Exhausting, Insufferable Narcissists
• Notes From The Edge Of The Narrative Matrix •

My God Israel supporters are exhausting. I've never gotten used to it.

"Wahh, Zohran Mamdani wants to murder Jews!"

"Wahh, the musician hurt the IDF's feelings!"

Shut up. Shut up. Shut the whole entire fuck up. Everyone is sick of your bullshit.

There is a genocide happening. A genocide. Babies are being starved. IDF soldiers are telling the Israeli press that they're being ordered to massacre desperately hungry civilians at aid sites. There are vast stretches of the Gaza Strip that now look like the surface of the moon. Trump and Netanyahu are openly working to purge the Palestinian territory of Palestinians so the land can be permanently taken from them.

Your feelings don't matter. The world does not revolve around you and your feelings. Your emotional response to whatever made up nonsense you're choosing to have a melodramatic tantrum about today is completely irrelevant. Every single Palestinian who died today, individually, matters infinitely more than every feeling you've ever felt about every imaginary phantom you've pretended to feel threatened by.

Anyone who has had the misfortune of knowing a manipulative narcissist has seen all these patterns before. The self-centeredness. The hypocrisy. The horrific abuse, followed by collapsing into blubbering victimhood the second the abuse is called out. The aggressive efforts to control the narrative and frame all critics and rivals as evil monsters. It's a very familiar playbook.

My hope for our world is that we one day become so emotionally and psychologically healthy that such cynical manipulations stand out like a white cloud against a deep blue sky. That we become so caring, understanding and supportive of our fellow human beings that the needful get everything they require to lead a fulfilling life, while sociopathy and psychopathy become as alienating and disadvantageous as chronic schizophrenia is today. That we become so tender-hearted that genocide can never rear its ugly head on this planet again, and all the abusive dynamics which made the Gaza holocaust possible fade away like darkness in the rising sun.

•

The real story is not that one musical act said "death to the IDF" at Glastonbury Festival, the real story is that a huge number of acts spoke out in support of Palestine at Glastonbury Festival. They're just making the story about one of those acts hoping you won't notice that supporting Palestine and opposing Israel is what's popular and cool now.

•

It's so funny when people accuse me of "bias" when I talk about Gaza. Like oh no I'm not being neutral enough about the active genocide, I'm so sorry.

•

Israel is making it abundantly clear that it's going to keep doing everything it can to instigate a war between the US and Iran, and the Washington swamp is crawling with war sluts who are pushing in the same direction. Trump's cabinet is full of Iran hawks, and Trump himself has publicly confessed to being bought and owned by the world's richest Israeli, Miriam Adelson.

Israel will not stop pushing for a full-scale American regime change war until it gets it. It will keep pushing and pushing and pushing, because there's nothing stopping it from doing so. It has too much to gain and too little to lose, since the political layout in Official Washington and the parapolitical layout in the unelected deep state largely aligns with this goal as well. The warmongers will keep trying, and if they fail next time, they will try again.

Nobody with any real power is doing anything to permanently shut this warmongering down and lock it away; at most they're just postponing it a bit until the next moment of demented brinkmanship occurs.

What this means is that anyone in the United States who doesn't want this war to happen needs to get much, much more hostile toward all the elements that are seeking to bring it about. Support for Israel needs to become politically toxic. A complete abandonment of Washington's status quo approach to the middle east must be demanded. A robust peace movement needs to emerge.

The people in power aren't pushing back against this mad shove toward war, so the pushback is going to have to come from the American people themselves. It will not happen from the top down, so it's going to have to come from the bottom up, or it's not going to come at all. That's the only thing that will stop this looming nightmare from being inflicted upon our world. •

The Empire Has Accidentally Caused The Rebirth Of Real Counterculture In The West

Everyone's still talking about Bob Vylan, and rightly so. A crowd full of westerners happily being led through a chant of "Death, death to the IDF" at the 2025 Glastonbury Festival was a historical landmark moment for the 21st century, and the group's persecution at the hands of western governments is once again highlighting the way our society's purported values of free thought and free expression go right out the window wherever Israel is concerned.

But one thing that's not getting enough attention is the fact that many, many other acts also spoke out in support of Palestine at that same festival, and that the crowd was full of attendees waving Palestinian flags. Supporting Palestine and opposing Israel's genocidal atrocities is just what's cool now.

This is a massive cultural development, because it means we are seeing the emergence of actual, meaningful rebellion in western counterculture for the first time arguably since the Vietnam War. The artists and their fans aren't just talking the talk of sticking it to the establishment anymore.

For generations the ruling class has been successfully stomping out all politically relevant counterculture, first in the form of direct frontal assault by official government operations like COINTELPRO, and then by the way all major platforms and studios are owned by plutocrats who benefit from the imperial status quo and refuse to elevate anyone who might pose a threat to it.

There have of course been countless artists in every generation who put on a rebellious face and give the finger to authority, but they've never presented any kind of threat to real power. Punk rockers who sing "fuck the man" but never advance any actual tangible causes. Satanic panic bands and shock rock superstars scaring church ladies and stirring culture wars. Bands voicing criticisms of the Iraq invasion but making it about supporting the Democratic Party. Celebrity musicians promoting social justice and equality without ever saying anything that might inconvenience the oligarchs and empire managers who rule our world.

The rich and powerful don't care if you dye your hair or pierce your nose or kiss a member of the same sex or say Hail Satan. They don't care if you support one mainstream political faction over the other, or if you yell empty words about anarchy and revolution that aren't pointed toward any real material goals. They care very much, however, if you are undermining public consent for military and geopolitical agendas they've worked very hard to propagandize the public into accepting.

The establishment never dropped the hammer on Marilyn Manson. Lady Gaga never ran into trouble with the state for singing that gay people are Born This Way. Ozzy Osbourne is living in the lap of luxury with an estimated net worth of $220 million. But groups like Kneecap and Bob Vylan are being subjected to police investigations and visa revocations for taking a stand on Palestine.

Which, of course, is only going to make their position more popular among young people with a defiant streak in them.

It's hard to imagine how western governments could make support for Palestine look more attractive to western youths, really. Here's this unimaginably horrific mass atrocity that they can all watch unfolding on their phone screens in real time every single day of the year, and they're being told "You're not allowed to oppose this. We, the stuffed shirts in Washington and London, command you to obey. If you think unauthorized thoughts and chant unauthorized chants, we are going to get very huffy and upset."

I mean, can you think of anything more fun?

This is after all the generation who's been told that they need to accept being poorer and sicker than their parents and grandparents and that

they'll never own a home no matter what they do, knowing full well that the crusty old bastards finger-wagging at them for opposing an active genocide are the same freaks who've refused to do anything to steer their planet's ecosystem away from looming disaster. They have every reason to want to express defiance, and nothing to lose by doing so. •

A real, politically meaningful counterculture has been born in the western world, and our rulers are already showing us that they're afraid of it. This is a fascinating time to be alive. •

https://www.caitlinjohnst.one

www.ingramcontent.com/pod-product-compliance
Lightning Source LLC
Chambersburg PA
CBHW081203270326

41930CB00014B/3286